TRAIN YOUR BRAIN
CONCENTRATION

Published in 2023 by Welbeck
an imprint of Welbeck Non-Fiction,
part of the Welbeck Publishing Group
Offices in: London - 20 Mortimer Street, London W1T 3JW &
Sydney - Level 17, 207 Kent St, Sydney NSW 2000 Australia
www.welbeckpublishing.com

Puzzles and Design © 2023 Welbeck Non-Fiction,
part of Welbeck Publishing Group

Editorial: Conor Kilgallon
Design: Tall Tree Limited and Eliana Holder

A CIP catalogue for this book is available from the British
Library.

ISBN: 978-1-80279-561-5

Printed in China

10 9 8 7 6 5 4 3 2 1

TRAIN YOUR BRAIN
CONCENTRATION

200 EXERCISES TO MAINTAIN AND IMPROVE FOCUS

DR GARETH MOORE

WELBECK

CONTENTS

TRAIN YOUR BRAIN:
CONCENTRATION INTRODUCTION

Welcome to *Train Your Brain: Concentration*, packed from cover to cover with 200 puzzles and challenges of 25 highly varied types. They cover a wide range of activities, from logic puzzles through to observational tasks, and from number challenges through to creativity exercises.

The book is broken into eight separate chapters, and each chapter opens with some brain-training advice. This text covers a range of relevant topics, such as maintaining focus, setting goals, thinking logically and even extends to mindfulness techniques and ways to challenge yourself.

It's best to start at the beginning of the book and work your way through, since both the text and the puzzles evolve as you proceed. In particular, the chances are that you won't have come across several of the puzzle types in this book, so it's best to start with the easier ones in the initial chapters. Each type appears eight times, giving you a good chance to become familiar with the individual requirements and logic of each type of puzzle. The good news, however, is that your brain loves learning new skills, so as you learn to deal with these different types of puzzle you'll be racking up the mental benefits. And if at any point you find yourself confused as to the particular implications of the instructions for a puzzle, don't be afraid to take a look at its solution to work through how it fits with the rules as given. Note, however, that the creative tasks are open-ended, and so don't have fixed solutions since it's up to you how you fill them in.

Some of the puzzles might take a bit of practice to get the hang of, but try not to skip over the ones that you find extra tricky – these are probably the ones that will benefit you the most. Your brain thrives on new challenges, and the more novel and unusual a task the better. Similarly, don't avoid the creative challenges – they are designed to be highly constrained, so you shouldn't get stuck wondering 'where to start' with them. If you do, just pick up a pen or pencil and get going on them at random – as mentioned above, there are no right or wrong answers so you've really nothing to lose by trying them, and in return your brain will thank you for it. Start drawing, or shading, and just see what happens. Part of the way through the process some inspiration may strike!

When you get stuck on a logic puzzle, remember that it's okay to make an intelligent guess – or, failing that, even just a wild stab in the dark! As children we learn by experimenting, and it turns out this works really well for some puzzles too. It might even be the quickest way to learn to solve some of them, since your brain is great at spotting patterns – so just jump in and try something and see if it works.

Finally, while your brain does indeed love novelty it's important to also note that it doesn't learn well when frustrated. If you get truly stuck on a puzzle then don't be afraid to take a look at the solutions to 'borrow' a few extra clues to get you going again. It's better to complete a puzzle with help than to abandon it entirely!

Most of all, remember to have fun!

Dr Gareth Moore, London

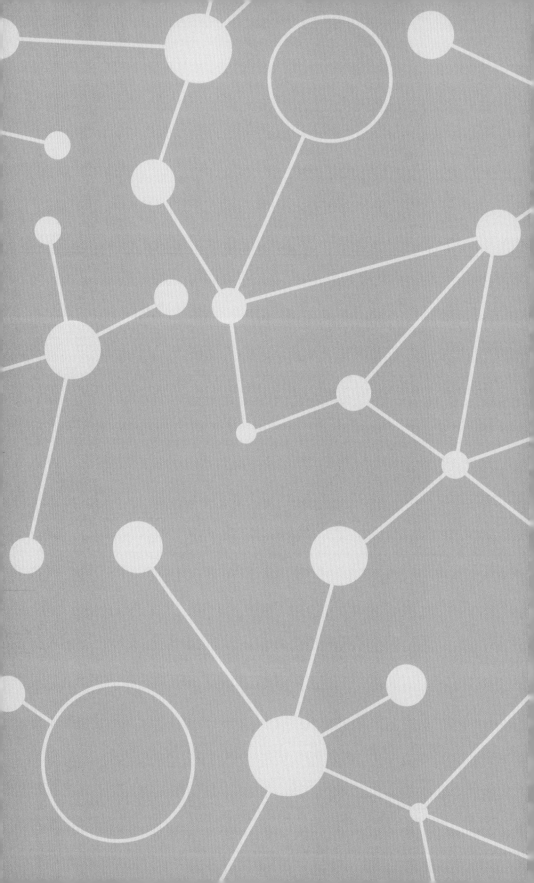

CHAPTER 1
MEET YOUR BRAIN

CHAPTER 1
MEET YOUR BRAIN

Whatever you've done today – from opening your eyes through to reading this book – your brain has been behind all of it, working away in the background without your conscious attention. But what, exactly, is your brain?

YOUR BRAIN IS POWERFUL

Your brain is largely made up of two different types of cell: neurons, also known as nerve cells, and glial cells. Glial cells are thought to mostly work as support cells for the neurons, while the neurons do the real hard-thinking work. The 100 billion or so neurons in your brain form connections to other neurons to create a complex network through which information can be captured, processed, and stored. In total, there are around 100 trillion of these connections in your brain, which gives you some idea as to just how much information your brain is capable of storing. What's more, these connections can each have an intricate set of requirements for when they become active, and information can flow not only forwards but also sometimes backwards too.

Your brain can be imagined as an insanely complex circuit board, with an amazing amount of processing power that makes it many times more efficient than any computer you might use. But your brain isn't a computer: it's a living, active organ which requires ongoing maintenance.

YOUR BRAIN IS FLEXIBLE

Your brain is constantly adapting to its surroundings, to learn about the world. Connections within the brain are continually being rebalanced, with those that help you being strengthened, while unused connections might be pruned away – just as muscles in your body lose strength if you don't use them frequently enough.

Throughout its lifetime, the brain goes through two major periods of change: one during infancy and the other during adolescence. Babies' brains are constantly growing and adapting to the vast amount of new stimuli encountered each day. In doing so, the brain makes a vast amount of connections, many of which it won't eventually need. The adolescent brain corrects this by starting a vast 'decluttering' process by getting rid of unused connections and rewiring itself for greater efficiency. If you ever wanted to know why teenagers sleep so much, that's the reason: their brains are busy undertaking a serious cerebral spring clean. It's also why it's much easier to learn things when you're really young, before your brain has discarded connections it thinks it won't need.

YOUR BRAIN NEEDS YOU

You should look after your brain just as much as you should look after the rest of your body.

- **Keep Fit:** Your brain depends on oxygen to work. Keeping physically fit will ensure that your brain has a quick and reliable oxygen supply – which literally will help you think faster.
- **Feed It:** Make sure you're getting all the vitamins, minerals and fatty acids your brain requires. A varied, healthy diet will allow your brain to get the food it needs to perform at its best – and don't rely entirely on vitamin pills.
- **Challenge It:** Your brain thrives on new experiences, and puzzling is a great way to present it with new and diverse challenges.

And with all this in mind, it's time to fire up some neurons and get puzzling.

1 SUDOKU

Place a digit from 1 to 9 into each empty square, so that no digit repeats in any row, column or bold-lined 3×3 box.

		4				2		
			2	9	8			
3								5
	8		6	5	3		4	
	7		9		4		6	
	9		8	1	7		3	
9								6
			1	7	2			
		1				4		

Solution on page 186

2 NO FOUR IN A ROW

Place either an 'X' or an 'O' into each empty square so that no lines of four or more 'X's or 'O's are formed in any direction, including diagonally.

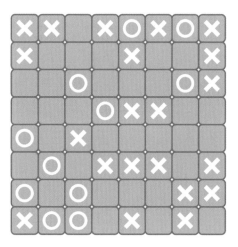

Solution on page 186

BRAIN CHAINS

Start with the number on the left of each chain, then apply each operation in turn until you reach the 'RESULT' box, writing your answer in the space provided. Try to complete the entire chain without using a calculator or making any written notes.

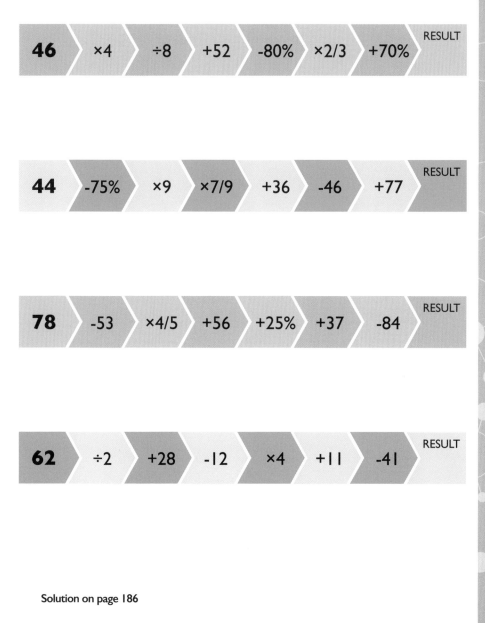

| 46 | ×4 | ÷8 | +52 | -80% | ×2/3 | +70% | RESULT |

| 44 | -75% | ×9 | ×7/9 | +36 | -46 | +77 | RESULT |

| 78 | -53 | ×4/5 | +56 | +25% | +37 | -84 | RESULT |

| 62 | ÷2 | +28 | -12 | ×4 | +11 | -41 | RESULT |

Solution on page 186

4 # JOIN THE DOTS

Join these dots in whatever way you like to create a doodle, abstract pattern or simple picture. If inspiration doesn't immediately strike, try drawing a few straight lines at random and then take a step back to see if the result reminds you of anything. Then continue in a similar vein.

5 # MISSING CUBE FACE

Which of the five given options should replace the white face, so that all four cube images could then be different views of exactly the same cube?

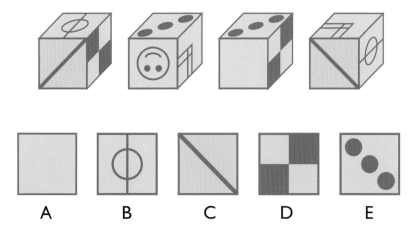

A   B   C   D   E

Solution on page 186

MAZE

Find your way from the top to the bottom of the maze. Some paths
pass under or over other paths.

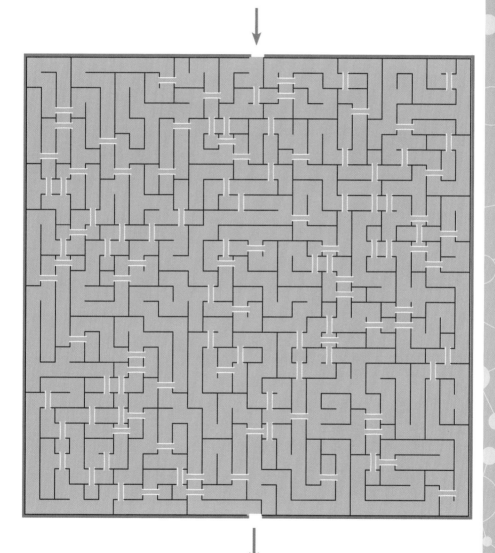

Solution on page 186

7 DOMINOES

Draw solid lines to divide the grid into a regular set of 0 to 6 dominoes, with exactly one of each domino. A '0' represents a blank on a traditional domino. Use the check-off chart to help you keep track of which dominoes you've already placed.

2	2	0	0	0	1	5	3
0	4	2	2	2	3	1	1
5	6	6	5	4	1	0	0
1	6	5	5	4	6	3	2
6	5	6	1	4	6	6	0
3	0	3	4	4	4	2	1
4	5	3	3	2	5	3	1

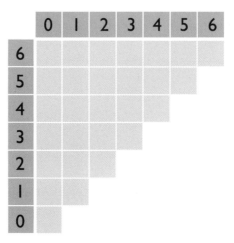

	0	1	2	3	4	5	6
6							
5							
4							
3							
2							
1							
0							

Solution on page 186

8 FENCES

Join all of the dots to form a single loop. The loop cannot cross or touch itself at any point. Only horizontal and vertical lines between dots are allowed. Some parts of the loop are already given.

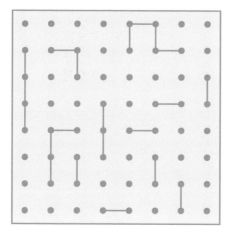

Solution on page 187

9 NUMBER PYRAMID

Complete this number pyramid by writing a number in each empty brick, so that each brick contains a value equal to the sum of the two bricks immediately beneath it.

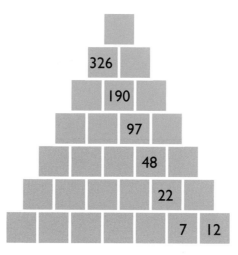

Solution on page 187

POETRY SLAM

Can you complete each of these two-line poems, in which only the first line is given? It's entirely up to you what you write, and they don't necessarily have to rhyme.

If only I could climb this tree,

....

When summer rain falls on the snow,

....

Flying round the world shows me,

....

 11

CUTTING PROBLEM

Draw along some of the dashed grid lines in order to divide this shape up into four regions. The regions must all be identical, although they may be rotated (but not reflected) relative to one another.

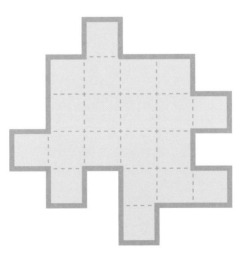

Solution on page 187

12 NUMBER PATH

Write a number in each empty square so that each number from 1 to 64 appears once in the grid. The numbers must form a path from 1 to 64, moving to a square one higher in value at each step as a king moves in chess: left, right, up, down or diagonally.

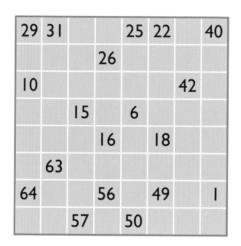

Solution on page 187

13 TRAIN TRACKS

Draw track pieces in some squares to complete a track that travels all the way from its entrance in the leftmost column to its exit in the bottom row. It can't otherwise exit the grid, and nor can it cross itself. Numbers outside the grid reveal the number of track pieces in each row and column. Every track piece must either go straight or turn a right-angled corner.

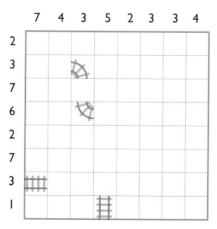

Solution on page 187

14 KAKURO

Place a number from 1 to 9 into each empty square, so that each continuous horizontal or vertical run of white squares adds up to the total given to its left or at its top, respectively. No number can repeat within any run.

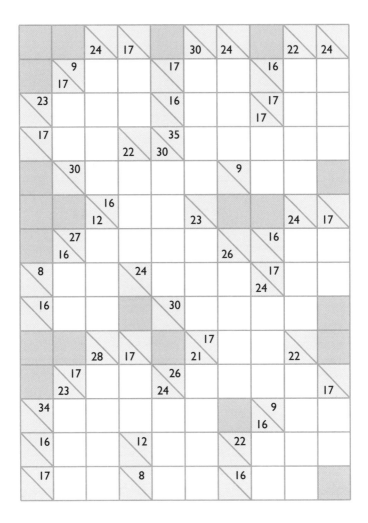

Solution on page 187

15 PIXEL ART

Shade in your choice of squares on each of these four canvases to create four simple pictures.

ODD-CUBE OUT

Imagine folding the shape below to form a six-sided cube. Which one of the five given cube pictures could not be the result?

Solution on page 187

PAIRED UP

Join these images into four identical pairs.

A

E

B

F

C

G

D

H

Solution on page 188

TOUCHY

Place a letter in the range A to H into each empty square in such a way that no letter repeats in any row or column. Additionally, identical letters may not be in diagonally touching squares.

			E	C			
		H			F		
	E					B	
G			D	E			C
A			F	G			D
	F					E	
		A			H		
			B	A			

Solution on page 188

19

SHAPE LINK

Draw a series of separate paths, each connecting a pair of identical shapes. No more than one path can enter any square, and paths can only travel horizontally or vertically between squares.

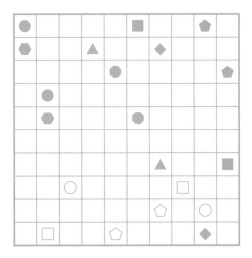

Solution on page 188

NUMBER DARTS

Form each of the given totals by choosing one number from each ring of the dartboard, so that those three numbers sum to the desired total.

TOTALS:	60
	67
	82

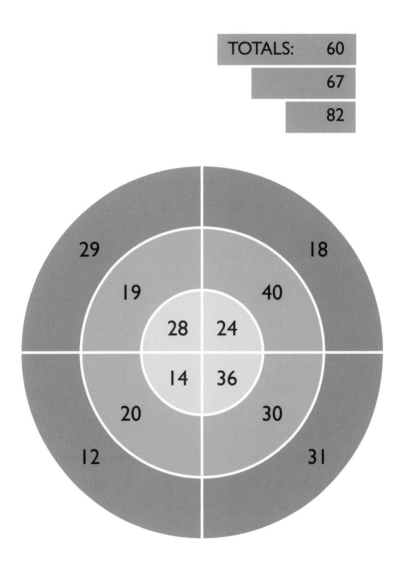

Solution on page 188

21 SHADING IT

Colour or shade in the regions formed by these shapes in whatever pattern or design you like. It's entirely up to you.

SPOT THE DIFFERENCE

Can you find all 8 differences between these two images?

Solution on page 189

CUBE COUNTING

How many cubes have been used to build the structure shown? You should assume that all 'hidden' cubes are present, and that it started off as a perfect 4x4x4 arrangement of cubes before any cubes were removed. There are no floating cubes.

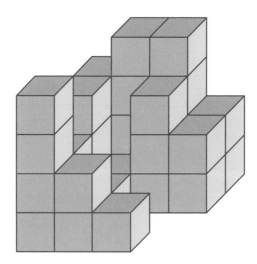

Solution on page 188

 # NUMBER ANAGRAMS

Use all five numbers and all four basic mathematical signs, +, -, x and ÷ (once each), to reach each of the three targets in turn. You can use as many brackets as you want, but you cannot create any fractional (non-integer) numbers during your calculation.

TARGETS:

A: 36   B: 52   C: 105

Solution on page 188

3D SUDOKU

Place 1 to 9 into each empty square, so no digit repeats in any row, column or black-lined 3x3 area. The rows and columns bend to follow the contours of the 3D shape, starting and ending at either the edge of the puzzle or at a thick bold line.

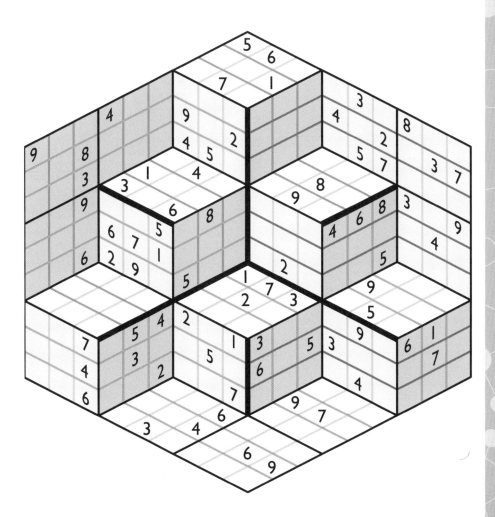

Solution on page 189

CHAPTER 2
KEEP IT BUSY

CHAPTER 2
KEEP IT BUSY

Your brain is always busy, and it's always learning. With every event we experience, our brains learn more about how the world works – and not just the way it does work, but also all the many ways in which it doesn't.

Your brain continually learns from and stores a vast amount of information to help you make smarter choices in the future, and solve related problems more efficiently when you next come to them. And what's more, it performs this amazing high-speed processing all without any conscious help from you. So, your brain is always learning and therefore in a constant state of training. But why then should we make the effort to do any further, more deliberate brain training?

KEEP IT VARIED

If you challenged yourself to make a hundred balloon animals every day for a year, you'd become very skilled and efficient at that specific task. Practising that specific skill, however, probably won't make you any better at such day-to-day tasks as remembering the groceries you meant to buy, or working out how much those groceries should cost.

The same is true of brain training. If you only ever solve sudoku puzzles, for example, then you'll get really good at sudoku – and perhaps related puzzles – but at some point your overall improvement in solving sudoku puzzles is likely to plateau. It's therefore important to continually challenge yourself with a wide variety of tasks. Indeed, your brain learns the most of all whenever it encounters new situations, requiring your diverse toolbox of experience to tackle uncharted territory. So the key to good brain training is variety and keeping things fresh.

With this in mind, you won't find endless, back-to-back repeats of the same puzzle type in this book. Instead, you'll need to use a variety of skills to tackle each new challenge as you work your way through, and you'll help keep different parts of your brain in action as you do so. If puzzles were brain food, then this book provides the kind of healthy, varied diet that can help yours to thrive.

Bear in mind that variety is also important to make sure you don't lose the skills you've already learned. For example, a bilingual person who only regularly speaks one language might find themselves forgetting words or expressions in their other, less-practised language. Similarly, it's important to make as wide-ranging use of your mental skills as possible, so they all stay in polished, tip-top condition.

KEEP IT RELAXED

Stressed brains don't learn efficiently, so the mental challenges you set yourself will offer more benefits if they are both fun and relaxing. This is one reason why puzzles are such a great choice. But pushing on with a puzzle that you're stuck on – to the point of becoming frustrated in the process – won't create the ideal conditions for you to learn effectively, and probably won't help you solve the puzzle either. So, if at any point you find you've reached a 'mental block' in a puzzle, try taking a guess to see if it gets you going again. Try solving something else, or simply take a break. When you come back refreshed and reenergized, you might spot something hiding in plain sight that you didn't see before, and be able to finish what you started. Plus, don't forget you're your clever brain sometimes makes deductions without you consciously being aware of them, particularly while you sleep.

 **SUDOKU**

Place a digit from 1 to 9 into each empty square, so that no digit repeats in any row, column or bold-lined 3×3 box.

	2		3					
6	1					8	2	
	9		1	7				
	2	4		1	6			
			5	9		4	7	
			2	5			8	
	8	3					5	7
			6		2			

Solution on page 190

 NO FOUR IN A ROW

Place either an 'X' or an 'O' into each empty square so that no lines of four or more 'X's or 'O's are formed in any direction, including diagonally.

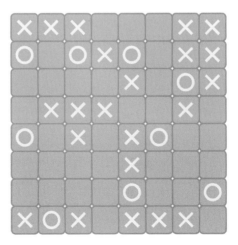

Solution on page 190

28 BRAIN CHAINS

Start with the number on the left of each chain, then apply each operation in turn until you reach the 'RESULT' box, writing your answer in the space provided. Try to complete the entire chain without using a calculator or making any written notes.

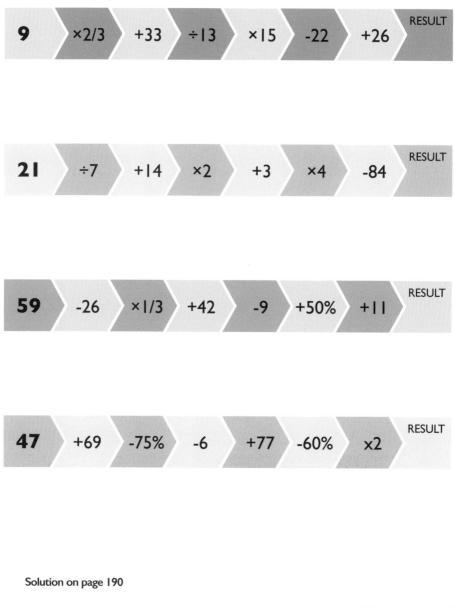

9 → ×2/3 → +33 → ÷13 → ×15 → -22 → +26 → RESULT

21 → ÷7 → +14 → ×2 → +3 → ×4 → -84 → RESULT

59 → -26 → ×1/3 → +42 → -9 → +50% → +11 → RESULT

47 → +69 → -75% → -6 → +77 → -60% → ×2 → RESULT

Solution on page 190

JOIN THE DOTS

Join these dots in whatever way you like, to create a doodle, abstract pattern or simple picture. If inspiration doesn't immediately strike, try drawing a few straight lines at random and then take a step back to see if the result reminds you of anything. Then continue in a similar vein.

MISSING CUBE FACE

Which of the five given options should replace the white face, so that all four cube images could then be different views of exactly the same cube?

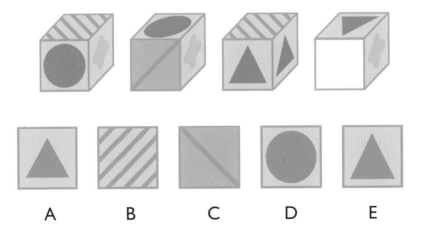

A   B   C   D   E

Solution on page 190

MAZE

Find your way from the top to the bottom of the maze. Some paths pass under or over other paths.

Solution on page 190

DOMINOES

Draw solid lines to divide the grid into a regular set of 0 to 6 dominoes, with exactly one of each domino. A '0' represents a blank on a traditional domino. Use the check-off chart to help you keep track of which dominoes you've already placed.

0	I	I	6	0	5	2	3
2	2	4	4	6	I	0	0
5	5	3	4	0	2	3	5
3	6	6	I	0	0	3	6
5	3	2	4	4	5	4	0
I	6	6	4	2	5	I	3
4	2	2	6	I	I	5	3

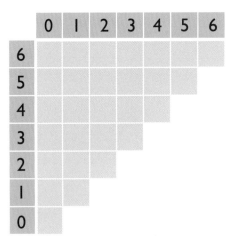

Solution on page 190

FENCES

Join all of the dots to form a single loop. The loop cannot cross or touch itself at any point. Only horizontal and vertical lines between dots are allowed. Some parts of the loop are already given.

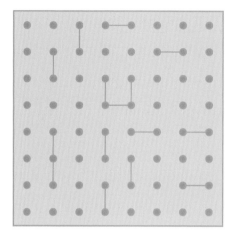

Solution on page 191

NUMBER PYRAMID

Complete this number pyramid by writing a number in each empty brick, so that each brick contains a value equal to the sum of the two bricks immediately beneath it.

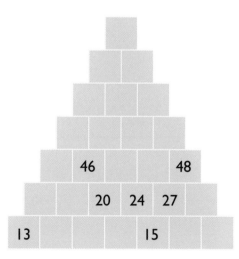

Solution on page 191

35 POETRY SLAM

Can you complete each of these two-line poems, in which only the
first line is given? It's entirely up to you what you write, and they don't
necessarily have to rhyme.

Standing on the plinth of shame,

....

Waiting for the coach to come,

....

Falling leaves lie all around,

....

36 CUTTING PROBLEM

Draw along some of the dashed grid lines in order to divide this shape
up into four regions. The regions must all be identical, although they may
be rotated (but not reflected) relative to one another.

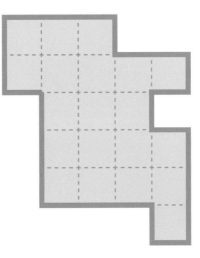

Solution on page 191

37 NUMBER PATH

Write a number in each empty square so that each number from 1 to 64 appears once in the grid. The numbers must form a path from 1 to 64, moving to a square one higher in value at each step as a king moves in chess: left, right, up, down or diagonally.

	10	5					
				46			
	17				47		
			28				50
24	55	1					
23	57				38		
	60				37		
64	63	61					36

Solution on page 191

38 TRAIN TRACKS

Draw track pieces in some squares to complete a track that travels all the way from its entrance in the leftmost column to its exit in the bottom row. It can't otherwise exit the grid, and nor can it cross itself. Numbers outside the grid reveal the number of track pieces in each row and column. Every track piece must either go straight or turn a right-angled corner.

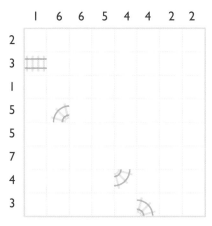

Solution on page 191

KAKURO

Place a number from 1 to 9 into each empty square, so that each continuous horizontal or vertical run of white squares adds up to the total given to its left or at its top, respectively. No number can repeat within any run.

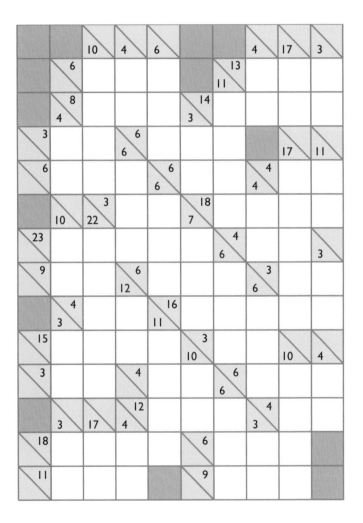

Solution on page 191

PIXEL ART

Shade in your choice of squares on each of these four canvases to create four simple pictures.

41 ODD-CUBE OUT

Imagine folding the shape below to form a six-sided cube. Which one of the five given cube pictures could not be the result?

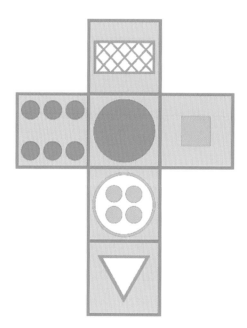

A 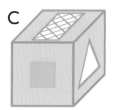   B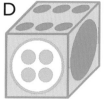

C 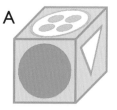   D 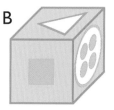   E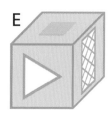

Solution on page 191

42 PAIRED UP

Join these images into four identical pairs.

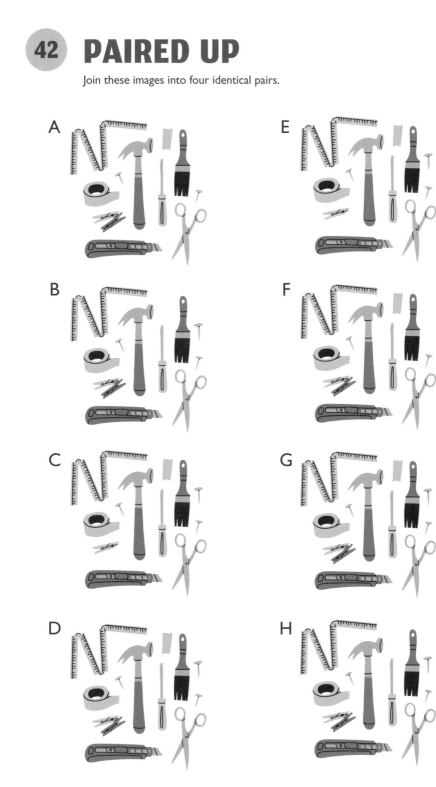

Solution on page 192

43 TOUCHY

Place a letter in the range A to H into each empty square in such a way that no letter repeats in any row or column. Additionally, identical letters may not be in diagonally touching squares.

	H		D	A		G	
B							A
			E	C			
C		G			D		E
D		E			B		G
			C	E			
E							H
	G		H	B		E	

Solution on page 192

 SHAPE LINK

44 SHAPE LINK

Draw a series of separate paths, each connecting a pair of identical shapes. No more than one path can enter any square, and paths can only travel horizontally or vertically between squares.

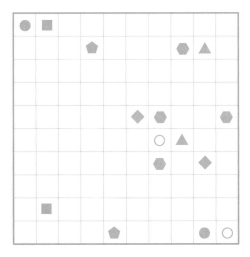

Solution on page 192

NUMBER DARTS

Form each of the given totals by choosing one number from each ring of the dartboard, so that those three numbers sum to the desired total.

TOTALS:	45
	53
	68

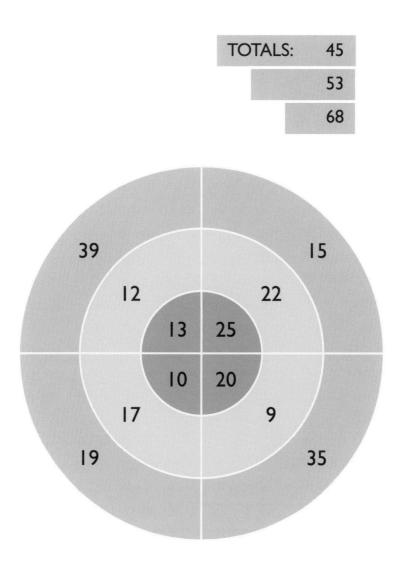

Solution on page 192

46 SHADING IT

Colour or shade in the regions formed by these shapes in whatever pattern or design you like. It's entirely up to you.

SPOT THE DIFFERENCE

Can you find all 8 differences between these two images?

Solution on page 193

48 CUBE COUNTING

How many cubes have been used to build the structure shown? You should assume that all 'hidden' cubes are present, and that it started off as a perfect 4x4x4 arrangement of cubes before any cubes were removed. There are no floating cubes.

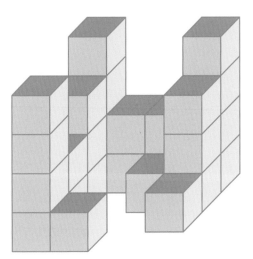

Solution on page 192

---

49 NUMBER ANAGRAMS

Use all five numbers and all four basic mathematical signs, +, -, x and ÷ (once each), to reach each of the three targets in turn. You can use as many brackets as you want, but you cannot create any fractional (non-integer) numbers during your calculation.

TARGETS:

A: 41   B: 107   C: 260

Solution on page 192

50 3D SUDOKU

Place 1 to 9 into each empty square, so no digit repeats in any row, column or black-lined 3x3 area. The rows and columns bend to follow the contours of the 3D shape, starting and ending at either the edge of the puzzle or at a thick bold line.

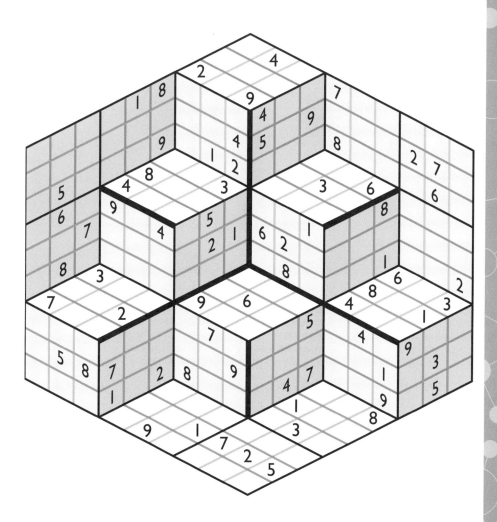

Solution on page 193

CHAPTER 3
MULTI-TASKING

CHAPTER 3
MULTI-TASKING

Your brain is great at multi-tasking, but you can only consciously think about one thing at a time. So, while you might be able to think through a recipe while stirring a pan, since the action of stirring the pan won't require much conscious attention, you'd struggle to do this while also solving a riddle. Those who claim to be great at multi-tasking are, in truth, really just great at switching between tasks efficiently, although you can nonetheless process input from different senses simultaneously – which is why you can, for example, carry on a conversation while driving, at least until you really need to concentrate on that driving.

REMOVE DISTRACTIONS

Distractions are everywhere. In a world full of technology, we are never far away from a phone call, email notification or text message ready to draw our focus away from whatever we were working on. Distractions can be sounds, such as other people talking or a doorbell sounding, or they can be visual, such as someone walking past or whatever's on a TV screen. They can also be physical, such as the tempting smell of food, or an annoying draught from a window.

So, whenever we need to get something done, we can make it easier for our brain by doing everything we reasonably can to remove unnecessary distractions. This can involve such simple tasks as:

- Closing doors and windows to minimize distracting noises and draughts
- Switching off unnecessary electronics or putting them into silent mode
- Making sure you are in a comfortable working position
- Adjusting room temperatures – or clothing – so you are neither too hot or cold

- Finding somewhere you are less likely to be disturbed by other people
- Removing tempting food from your workspace, to avoid distracting aromas – and hunger!

ENABLE FOCUS

Once you've eliminated external distractions, it's time to remove internal ones by trying to maintain focus.

It can be very easy to lose concentration by letting your thoughts drift to an unrelated task you might be facing, and while it can be hard to avoid this entirely, there are certain techniques that can help. One method in particular is to simply make a quick note of anything distracting that pops into your mind – this allows you to be sure you will remember to return to it later, so you don't need to worry about forgetting it. To get your original task done as efficiently as possible, try not to make unnecessary sidetracks into other tasks – while they may be quicker to finish, they won't help you with your original goal!

More generally, looking after your mental health can help you maintain the ability to stay calm and focused when you need to be. When you are anxious or stressed, it's harder for your brain to maintain focus, and you become less efficient as a result. Short-term stress can be beneficial, but long-term stress is debilitating and may require professional medical advice to tackle.

If you find your mind overrun with competing thoughts, you could try simple meditation exercises to practise bringing your mind onto whatever it needs to attend to. These can be as simple as closing your eyes and taking a couple of deep breaths before you begin, to help clear your mind for the mental transition into the task.

SUDOKU

Place a digit from 1 to 9 into each empty square, so that no digit repeats in any row, column or bold-lined 3×3 box.

Solution on page 194

NO FOUR IN A ROW

Place either an 'X' or an 'O' into each empty square so that no lines of four or more 'X's or 'O's are formed in any direction, including diagonally.

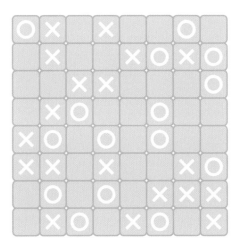

Solution on page 194

53 BRAIN CHAINS

Start with the number on the left of each chain, then apply each operation in turn until you reach the 'RESULT' box, writing your answer in the space provided. Try to complete the entire chain without using a calculator or making any written notes.

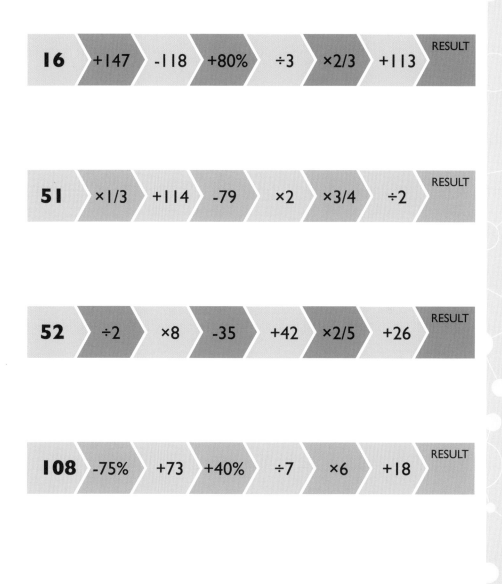

16 → +147 → -118 → +80% → ÷3 → ×2/3 → +113 → RESULT

51 → ×1/3 → +114 → -79 → ×2 → ×3/4 → ÷2 → RESULT

52 → ÷2 → ×8 → -35 → +42 → ×2/5 → +26 → RESULT

108 → -75% → +73 → +40% → ÷7 → ×6 → +18 → RESULT

Solution on page 194

54 JOIN THE DOTS

Join these dots in whatever way you like, to create a doodle, abstract pattern or simple picture. If inspiration doesn't immediately strike, try drawing a few straight lines at random and then take a step back to see if the result reminds you of anything. Then continue in a similar vein.

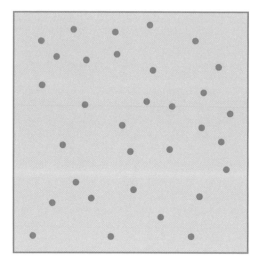

55 MISSING CUBE FACE

Which of the five given options should replace the white face, so that all four cube images could then be different views of exactly the same cube?

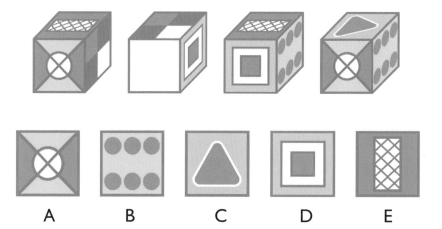

A   B   C   D   E

Solution on page 194

MAZE

Find your way from the top to the bottom of the maze. Some paths pass under or over other paths.

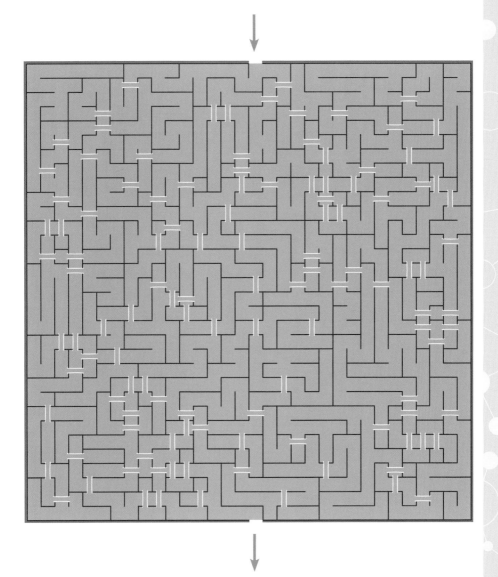

Solution on page 194

57 DOMINOES

Draw solid lines to divide the grid into a regular set of 0 to 6 dominoes, with exactly one of each domino. A '0' represents a blank on a traditional domino. Use the check-off chart to help you keep track of which dominoes you've already placed.

3	3	5	3	0	6	1	2
2	0	1	6	0	1	2	4
6	5	2	6	4	6	3	3
4	2	2	1	4	0	4	5
4	5	5	1	2	5	2	1
1	4	5	6	3	6	4	0
5	3	0	6	1	0	3	0

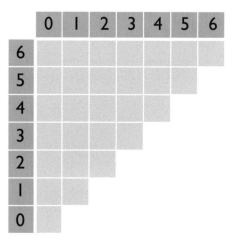

	0	1	2	3	4	5	6
6							
5							
4							
3							
2							
1							
0							

Solution on page 194

58 FENCES

Join all of the dots to form a single loop. The loop cannot cross or touch itself at any point. Only horizontal and vertical lines between dots are allowed. Some parts of the loop are already given.

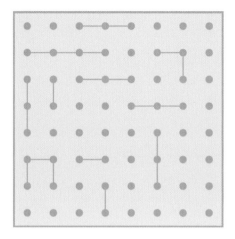

Solution on page 195

---

59 NUMBER PYRAMID

Complete this number pyramid by writing a number in each empty brick, so that each brick contains a value equal to the sum of the two bricks immediately beneath it.

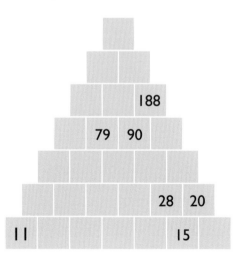

Solution on page 195

60 POETRY SLAM

Can you complete each of these two-line poems, in which only the first line is given? It's entirely up to you what you write, and they don't necessarily have to rhyme.

Once upon a Tuesday morn,

....

The river tumbled down the creek,

....

The ride span faster, faster, faster,

....

61 CUTTING PROBLEM

Draw along some of the dashed grid lines in order to divide this shape up into four regions. The regions must all be identical, although they may be rotated (but not reflected) relative to one another.

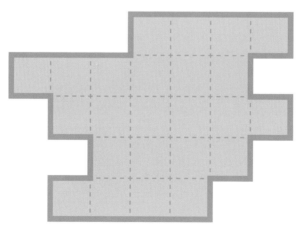

Solution on page 195

62 NUMBER PATH

Write a number in each empty square so that each number from 1 to 64 appears once in the grid. The numbers must form a path from 1 to 64, moving to a square one higher in value at each step as a king moves in chess: left, right, up, down or diagonally.

8	4			42			
	2		45	41			
		1					
15		32					
26	28		33			52	
		59					
22	60					50	
21			64				

Solution on page 195

---

63 TRAIN TRACKS

Draw track pieces in some squares to complete a track that travels all the way from its entrance in the leftmost column to its exit in the bottom row. It can't otherwise exit the grid, and nor can it cross itself. Numbers outside the grid reveal the number of track pieces in each row and column. Every track piece must either go straight or turn a right-angled corner.

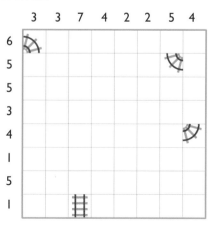

Solution on page 195

KAKURO

Place a number from 1 to 9 into each empty square, so that each continuous horizontal or vertical run of white squares adds up to the total given to its left or at its top, respectively. No number can repeat within any run.

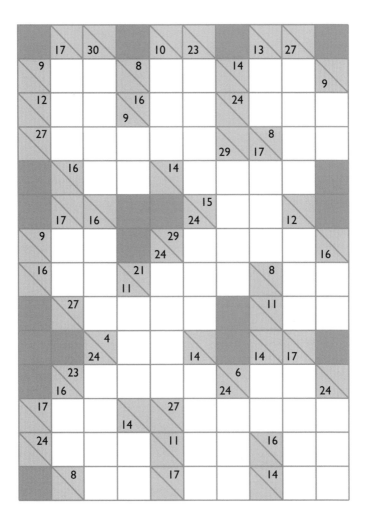

Solution on page 195

PIXEL ART

Shade in your choice of squares on each of these two canvases to create two simple pictures.

ODD-CUBE OUT

Imagine folding the shape below to form a six-sided cube. Which one of the five given cube pictures could not be the result?

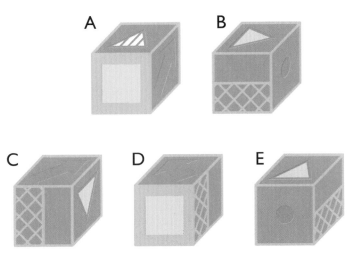

Solution on page 195

67 PAIRED UP

Join these images into four identical pairs.

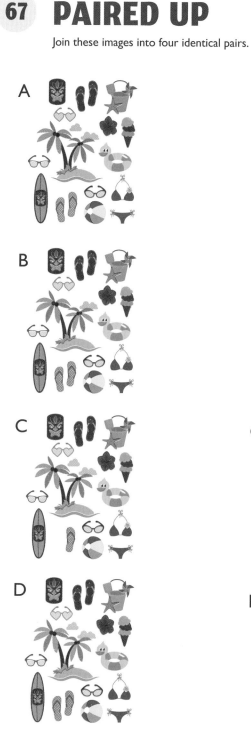

Solution on page 196

TOUCHY

Place a letter in the range A to H into each empty square in such a way that no letter repeats in any row or column. Additionally, identical letters may not be in diagonally touching squares.

	H					F	
F			E	B			H
			H	F			
	F	C			G	D	
	D	G			B	A	
			D	G			
D			B	A			E
	E					B	

Solution on page 196

 # SHAPE LINK

Draw a series of separate paths, each connecting a pair of identical shapes. No more than one path can enter any square, and paths can only travel horizontally or vertically between squares.

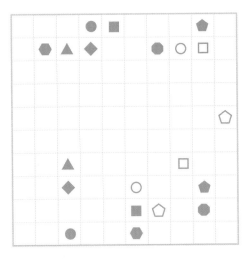

Solution on page 196

NUMBER DARTS

Form each of the given totals by choosing one number from each ring of the dartboard, so that those three numbers sum to the desired total.

TOTALS: 48
66
77

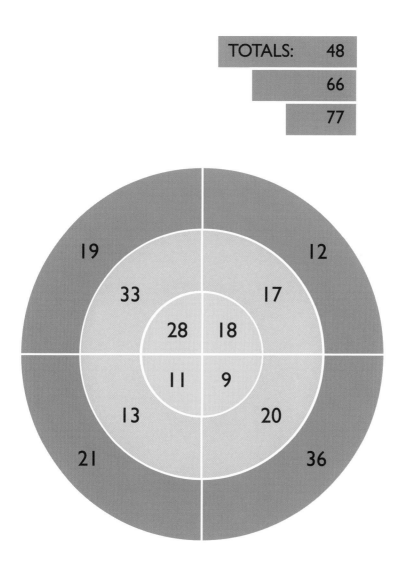

Solution on page 196

71 SHADING IT

Colour or shade in the regions formed by these shapes in whatever pattern or design you like. It's entirely up to you.

SPOT THE DIFFERENCE

Can you find all 8 differences between these two images?

Solution on page 197

73 CUBE COUNTING

How many cubes have been used to build the structure shown? You should assume that all 'hidden' cubes are present, and that it started off as a perfect 5x4x4 arrangement of cubes before any cubes were removed. There are no floating cubes.

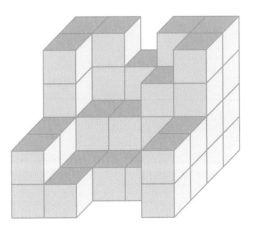

Solution on page 196

74 NUMBER ANAGRAMS

Use all five numbers and all four basic mathematical signs, +, -, x and ÷ (once each), to reach each of the three targets in turn. You can use as many brackets as you want, but you cannot create any fractional (non-integer) numbers during your calculation.

TARGETS:

A: 25   B: 61   C: 107

Solution on page 196

75 3D SUDOKU

Place 1 to 9 into each empty square, so no digit repeat in any row, column or black-lined 3x3 area. The rows and columns bend to follow the contours of the 3D shape, starting and ending at either the edge of the puzzle or at a thick bold line.

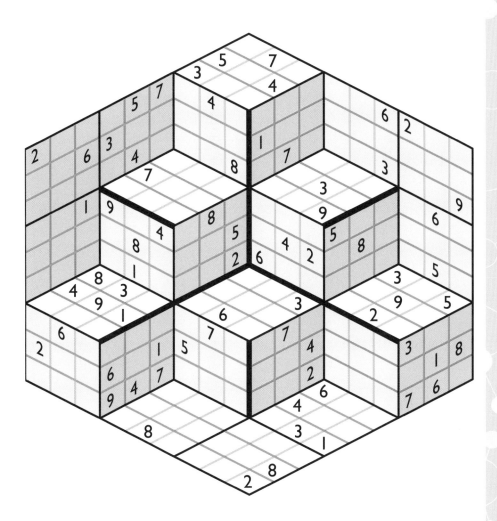

Solution on page 197

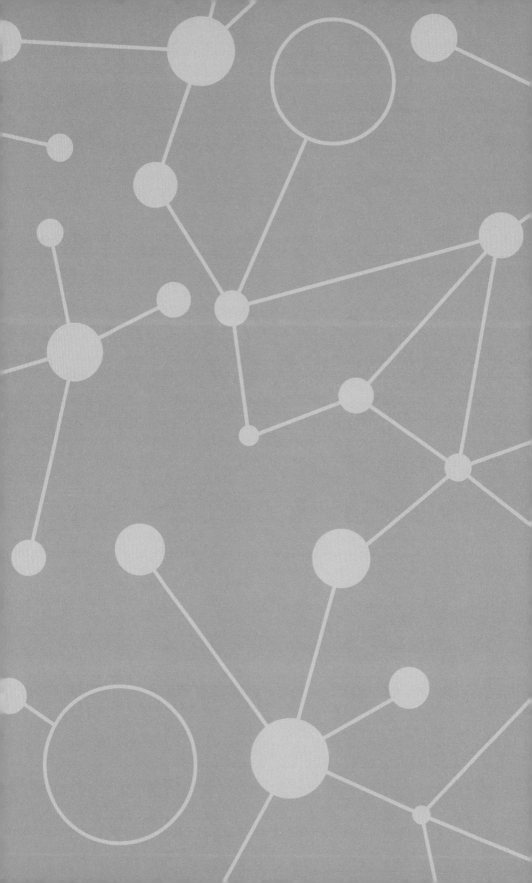

CHAPTER 4
SETTING GOALS

CHAPTER 4
SETTING GOALS

How can you turn dreams into reality? And how can you keep up with your work or school deadlines?

Whatever it is that you want to achieve in life – whether it's putting up a shelf or flying to the moon – dreams will often remain dreams if you don't come up with a plan and take some solid steps towards achieving these aims. Large projects can be daunting, but with a reasonable plan and a well-trained mind, there's no reason you shouldn't be able to organize your way to success. Here are some tips to help you plan for – and achieve – your goals:

- **Make a Plan:** Work out what needs to be done and think about the steps that you need to complete in order to achieve it, whether that's buying wood for a shelf or picking the right subjects to study. Decide to prioritise the things you care most about and put other objectives on the back burner. Write out a list of all the things you want to achieve and then order it according to priority.

- **Break It Down:** Breaking a large task down into multiple smaller tasks will almost always make it seem less intimidating, since smaller tasks feel inherently more achievable. You'll get a mental boost every time you tick off each of these subtasks, and you'll be able to more directly track your progress to completing the whole thing. It might also help you assign your time more sensibly.

- **Get Going:** Reluctance towards starting a task can hold you back from completing it effectively, or even at all. Often, it doesn't matter where you start with a challenge, just so long as you do start. If you're writing an essay – or a book – try starting at the end, or in the middle, and come back to the beginning later. Once you get going on a task, you may find yourself 'in the zone' and more able to tackle the parts you found tricky.

- **Don't Aim For 100% Perfection:** It's better to achieve your goal than not achieve it, so while it's good to try, it can sometimes be bad to try too much. Usually, it's only necessary to do something well enough – you don't have to do everything to the absolute extreme of your ability, particularly if it detracts from both your own enjoyment and perhaps even that of others.

- **Be Realistic:** Make sure that your goal is achievable. Do you have enough time to be able to complete it? Is it physically possible to actually do it? Are you too old/young, or ineligible in some other way? Once you know that your objective is definitely within your reach, you'll have the motivation to keep going when it gets tough.

- **Allow a Margin for Error:** Few significant projects will progress without any setbacks, no matter how well you plan. Accept that you may sometimes struggle with temporary hitches, or with tasks that turn out to be tricker than anticipated. Stay focused, keep going, and reformulate your plan if necessary.

- **Reward Yourself:** Make time to acknowledge your progress, and celebrate small achievements along the way. That might be as simple as taking a short break, or crossing something off the list with your favourite pen. It's helpful to associate hard work with feeling good!

76 SUDOKU

Place a digit from 1 to 9 into each empty square, so that no digit repeats in any row, column or bold-lined 3×3 box.

	4		6		1		8	
	5	1				2	9	
		7				3		
			1	2	7			
7			3		4			2
			5	8	9			
		3				9		
	7	8				5	1	
	2		9		5		7	

Solution on page 198

---

77 NO FOUR IN A ROW

Place either an 'X' or an 'O' into each empty square so that no lines of four or more 'X's or 'O's are formed in any direction, including diagonally.

Solution on page 198

78 BRAIN CHAINS

Start with the number on the left of each chain, then apply each operation in turn until you reach the 'RESULT' box, writing your answer in the space provided. Try to complete the entire chain without using a calculator or making any written notes.

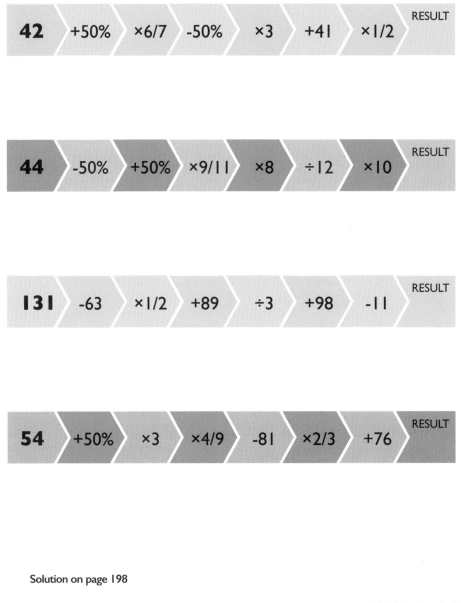

42 → +50% → ×6/7 → -50% → ×3 → +41 → ×1/2 → RESULT

44 → -50% → +50% → ×9/11 → ×8 → ÷12 → ×10 → RESULT

131 → -63 → ×1/2 → +89 → ÷3 → +98 → -11 → RESULT

54 → +50% → ×3 → ×4/9 → -81 → ×2/3 → +76 → RESULT

Solution on page 198

JOIN THE DOTS

Join these dots in whatever way you like, to create a doodle, abstract pattern or simple picture. If inspiration doesn't immediately strike, try drawing a few straight lines at random and then take a step back to see if the result reminds you of anything. Then continue in a similar vein.

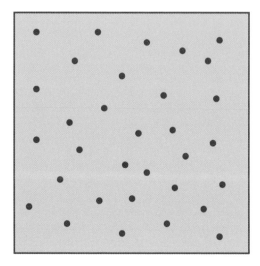

 MISSING CUBE FACE

Which of the five given options should replace the white face, so that all four cube images could then be different views of exactly the same cube?

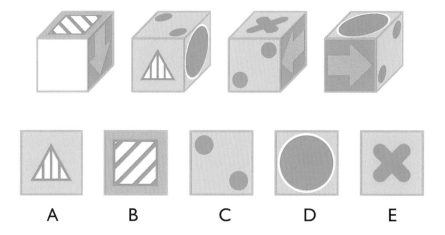

A B C D E

Solution on page 198

81 MAZE

Find your way from the top to the bottom of the maze. Some paths pass under or over other paths.

Solution on page 198

DOMINOES

Draw solid lines to divide the grid into a regular set of 0 to 6 dominoes, with exactly one of each domino. A '0' represents a blank on a traditional domino. Use the check-off chart to help you keep track of which dominoes you've already placed.

6	2	5	4	6	3	4	3
0	5	6	6	2	1	1	3
0	1	0	4	4	3	3	4
5	0	2	6	1	6	0	4
6	2	2	0	5	2	1	3
4	4	1	2	0	6	2	3
5	3	1	5	5	5	1	0

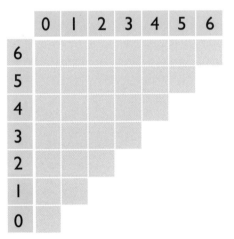

Solution on page 198

83 FENCES

Join all of the dots to form a single loop. The loop cannot cross or touch itself at any point. Only horizontal and vertical lines between dots are allowed. Some parts of the loop are already given.

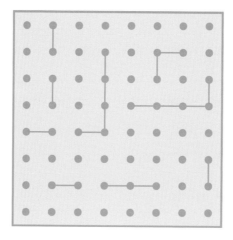

Solution on page 199

84 NUMBER PYRAMID

Complete this number pyramid by writing a number in each empty brick, so that each brick contains a value equal to the sum of the two bricks immediately beneath it.

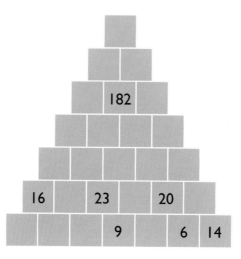

Solution on page 199

85 POETRY SLAM

Can you complete each of these two-line poems, in which only the first line is given? It's entirely up to you what you write, and they don't necessarily have to rhyme.

The ruler looked out o'er the land,

....

She cried and cried then dried her eyes,

....

When I was just five or six,

....

86 CUTTING PROBLEM

Draw along some of the dashed grid lines in order to divide this shape up into four regions. The regions must all be identical, although they may be rotated (but not reflected) relative to one another.

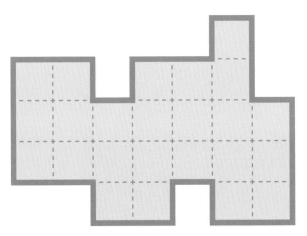

Solution on page 199

87 NUMBER PATH

Write a number in each empty square so that each number from 1 to 64 appears once in the grid. The numbers must form a path from 1 to 64, moving to a square one higher in value at each step as a king moves in chess: left, right, up, down or diagonally.

		38	37				
43				32		17	
	42	30					
45							14
	8						25
		3	4	64			
					61	60	59
1			52	53			

Solution on page 199

88 TRAIN TRACKS

Draw track pieces in some squares to complete a track that travels all the way from its entrance in the leftmost column to its exit in the bottom row. It can't otherwise exit the grid, and nor can it cross itself. Numbers outside the grid reveal the number of track pieces in each row and column. Every track piece must either go straight or turn a right-angled corner.

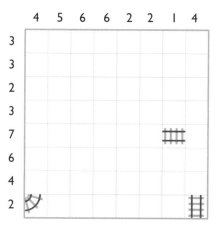

Solution on page 199

89 KAKURO

Place a number from 1 to 9 into each empty square, so that each continuous horizontal or vertical run of white squares adds up to the total given to its left or at its top, respectively. No number can repeat within any run.

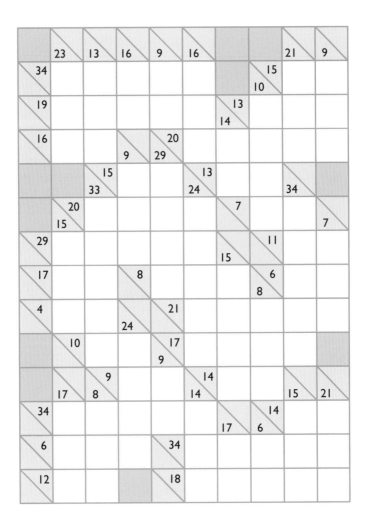

Solution on page 199

PIXEL ART

Shade in your choice of squares on each of these two canvases to create two simple pictures.

ODD-CUBE OUT

Imagine folding the shape below to form a six-sided cube. Which one of the five given cube pictures could not be the result?

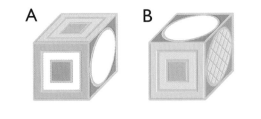

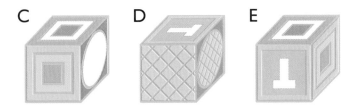

A   B

C   D   E

Solution on page 199

PAIRED UP

Join these images into four identical pairs.

A 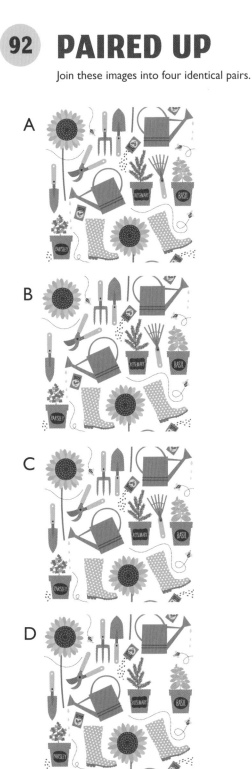 E

B

F

C

G

D

H

Solution on page 200

93 TOUCHY

Place a letter in the range A to H into each empty square in such a way that no letter repeats in any row or column. Additionally, identical letters may not be in diagonally touching squares.

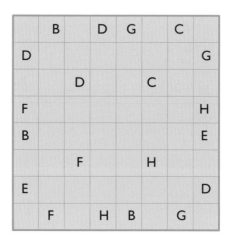

Solution on page 200

94 SHAPE LINK

Draw a series of separate paths, each connecting a pair of identical shapes. No more than one path can enter any square, and paths can only travel horizontally or vertically between squares.

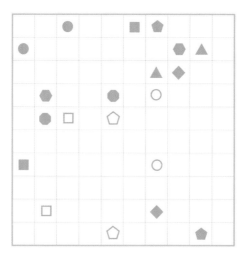

Solution on page 200

NUMBER DARTS

Form each of the given totals by choosing one number from each ring of the dartboard, so that those three numbers sum to the desired total.

TOTALS:	58
	74
	88

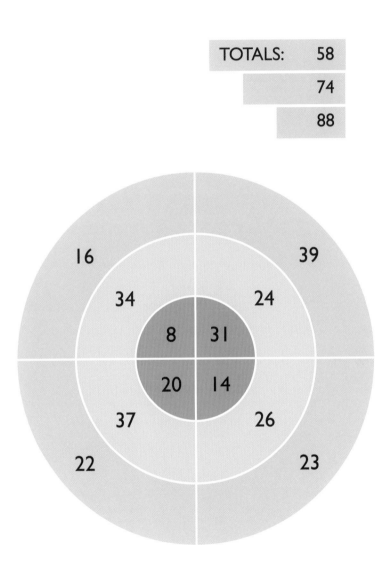

Solution on page 200

96 SHADING IT

Colour or shade in the regions formed by these shapes in whatever pattern or design you like. It's entirely up to you.

SPOT THE DIFFERENCE

Can you find all 8 differences between these two images?

Solution on page 201

 **CUBE COUNTING**

How many cubes have been used to build the structure shown? You should assume that all 'hidden' cubes are present, and that it started off as a perfect 5x4x4 arrangement of cubes before any cubes were removed. There are no floating cubes.

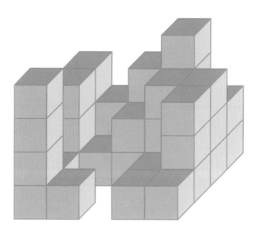

Solution on page 200

99 NUMBER ANAGRAMS

Use all five numbers and all four basic mathematical signs, +, -, x and ÷ (once each), to reach each of the three targets in turn. You can use as many brackets as you want, but you cannot create any fractional (non-integer) numbers during your calculation.

TARGETS:

A: 24   B: 98   C: 442

Solution on page 200

100 3D SUDOKU

Place 1 to 9 into each empty square, so no digit repeat in any row, column or black-lined 3x3 area. The rows and columns bend to follow the contours of the 3D shape, starting and ending at either the edge of the puzzle or at a thick bold line.

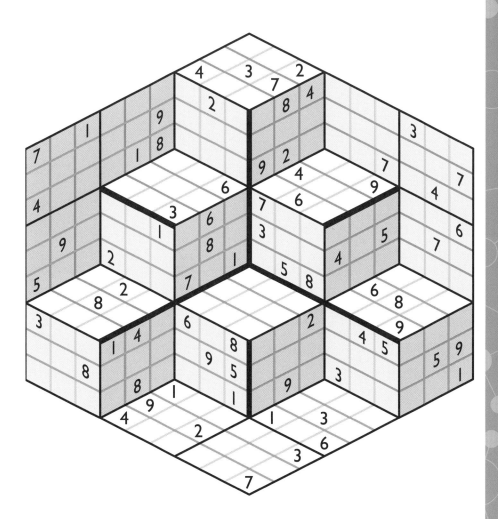

Solution on page 201

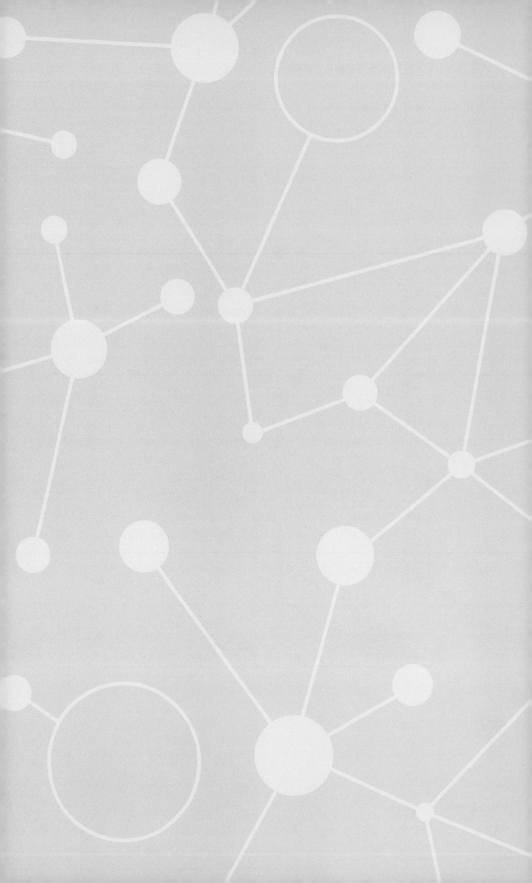

CHAPTER 5
CHALLENGE YOURSELF

CHAPTER 5
CHALLENGE YOURSELF

Did you know that fear of the unknown can stop you from unlocking your brain's full potential?

When you are young, you don't worry much about the risk of getting hurt – either physically or mentally – when you make a mistake. Anxiety doesn't get in the way of exploring how the world works, which is essential so that your brain can learn everything it needs for you to make sense of life. But as you get older, there's a natural tendency to become more risk averse, since it can feel that any perceived 'failure' would be far more significant – it might affect how others feel about us, or even our own self-esteem. As a result, in general, you may have become less likely to seek out the new experiences that you require in order to help keep your brain sharp.

Although being aware of failure can sometimes keep you safe, it can also get in the way of feeding your brain the rich and varied diet of experiences that it needs to keep functioning at its best. You might find yourself avoiding new or more challenging tasks in favour of those which feel more familiar and safe – such as, for example, by trying only puzzles that you already know how to solve – but that's not always to your brain's advantage. One of the best ways to keep your brain fit is to continually seek out new experiences, which can challenge it with unfamiliar situations where new kinds of thinking might be required.

Here are some ways you could challenge yourself. Some are small in scale, whereas others would require more time and commitment:

- Try a fruit or vegetable you've never eaten before. Take the time to notice how it smells, tastes and feels. Would you eat it again?

- Take a walk along your street and look for things you've never noticed or paid attention to before. If you're stuck, look up: we rarely observe much about what's above our head height, even in familiar environments.

- Read a book or even just watch a TV show that is outside your usual comfort zone, particularly if it contains unfamiliar language, scenarios or situations.

- Learn a new language. There are tutorials online and within apps, as well as plenty of books to help you get going. The more unlike your main language the new language is, the better! Most languages include their own unique concepts, which can't otherwise be easily expressed in other languages.

- Travel if you can. Placing yourself in entirely new environments is the ultimate experience for your brain. This doesn't have to involve going far – just to somewhere that isn't familiar.

Every new experience your brain encounters will challenge it with unfamiliar information and help build your overall mental capabilities. While most of us don't have the means to travel the world every day, there's nothing stopping you from seeking out just one new experience, however small, each and every day. You brain will definitely thank you for it.

101 SUDOKU

Place a digit from 1 to 9 into each empty square, so that no digit repeats in any row, column or bold-lined 3×3 box.

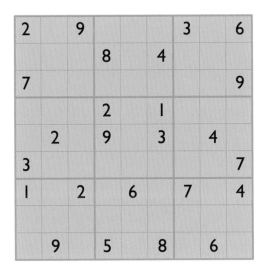

Solution on page 202

102 NO FOUR IN A ROW

Place either an 'X' or an 'O' into each empty square so that no lines of four or more 'X's or 'O's are formed in any direction, including diagonally.

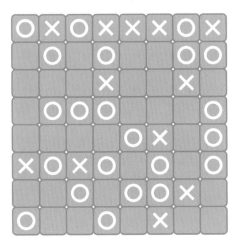

Solution on page 202

103 BRAIN CHAINS

Start with the number on the left of each chain, then apply each operation in turn until you reach the 'RESULT' box, writing your answer in the space provided. Try to complete the entire chain without using a calculator or making any written notes.

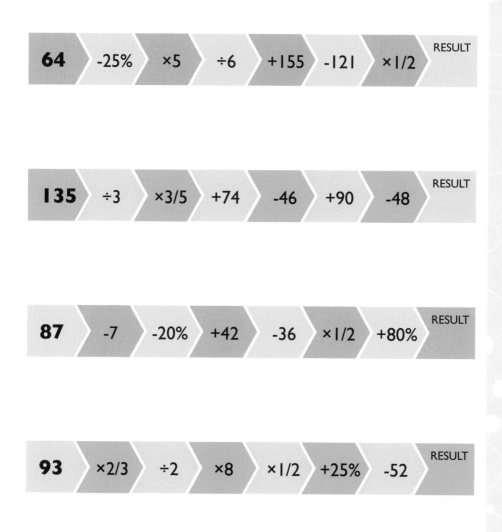

64 | -25% | ×5 | ÷6 | +155 | -121 | ×1/2 | RESULT

135 | ÷3 | ×3/5 | +74 | -46 | +90 | -48 | RESULT

87 | -7 | -20% | +42 | -36 | ×1/2 | +80% | RESULT

93 | ×2/3 | ÷2 | ×8 | ×1/2 | +25% | -52 | RESULT

Solution on page 202

JOIN THE DOTS

Join these dots in whatever way you like, to create a doodle, abstract pattern or simple picture. If inspiration doesn't immediately strike, try drawing a few straight lines at random and then take a step back to see if the result reminds you of anything. Then continue in a similar vein.

105 **MISSING CUBE FACE**

Which of the five given options should replace the white face, so that all four cube images could then be different views of exactly the same cube?

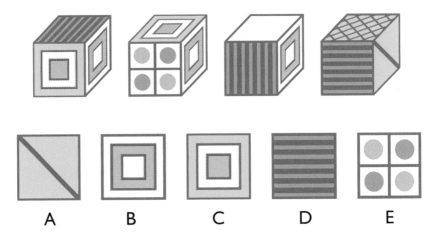

A   B   C   D   E

Solution on page 202

106 MAZE

Find your way from the top to the bottom of the maze. Some paths pass under or over other paths.

Solution on page 202

107 DOMINOES

Draw solid lines to divide the grid into a regular set of 0 to 6 dominoes, with exactly one of each domino. A '0' represents a blank on a traditional domino. Use the check-off chart to help you keep track of which dominoes you've already placed.

6	1	1	4	2	3	1	4
0	2	2	6	2	5	4	0
3	6	5	6	2	1	5	0
3	1	2	4	4	3	0	4
5	1	3	0	3	0	1	4
1	6	0	3	2	5	5	4
6	3	0	5	6	6	5	2

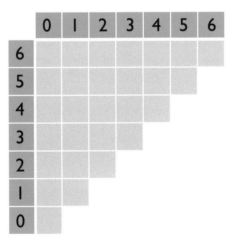

	0	1	2	3	4	5	6
6							
5							
4							
3							
2							
1							
0							

Solution on page 202

108 FENCES

Join all of the dots to form a single loop. The loop cannot cross or touch itself at any point. Only horizontal and vertical lines between dots are allowed. Some parts of the loop are already given.

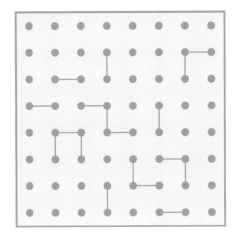

Solution on page 203

109 NUMBER PYRAMID

Complete this number pyramid by writing a number in each empty brick, so that each brick contains a value equal to the sum of the two bricks immediately beneath it.

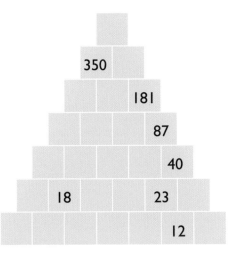

Solution on page 203

110 POETRY SLAM

Can you complete each of these two-line poems, in which only the first line is given? It's entirely up to you what you write, and they don't necessarily have to rhyme.

The tune he whistled carried far,

....

The moon shone brightly from on high,

....

Birdsong filled the midday air,

....

111 CUTTING PROBLEM

Draw along some of the dashed grid lines in order to divide this shape up into four regions. The regions must all be identical, although they may be rotated (but not reflected) relative to one another.

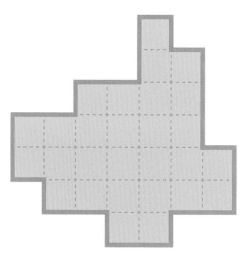

Solution on page 203

112 NUMBER PATH

Write a number in each empty square so that each number from 1 to
64 appears once in the grid. The numbers must form a path from 1 to
64, moving to a square one higher in value at each step as a king moves
in chess: left, right, up, down or diagonally.

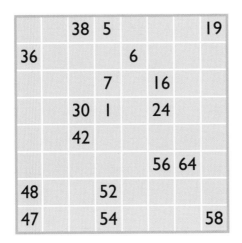

Solution on page 203

113 TRAIN TRACKS

Draw track pieces in some squares to complete a track that travels
all the way from its entrance in the leftmost column to its exit in the
bottom row. It can't otherwise exit the grid, and nor can it cross itself.
Numbers outside the grid reveal the number of track pieces in each
row and column. Every track piece must either go straight or turn a
right-angled corner.

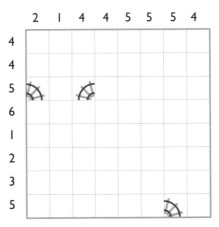

Solution on page 203

KAKURO

Place a number from 1 to 9 into each empty square, so that each
continuous horizontal or vertical run of white squares adds up to the
total given to its left or at its top, respectively. No number can repeat
within any run.

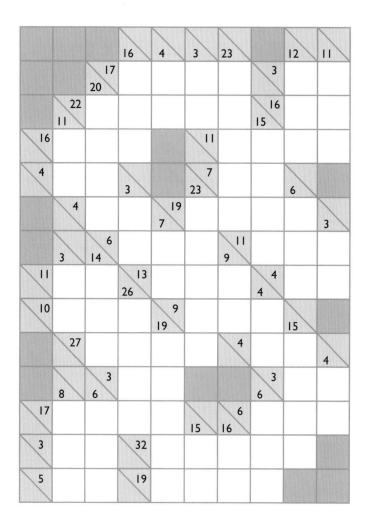

Solution on page 203

115 PIXEL ART

Shade in your choice of squares on this canvas to create a simple picture.

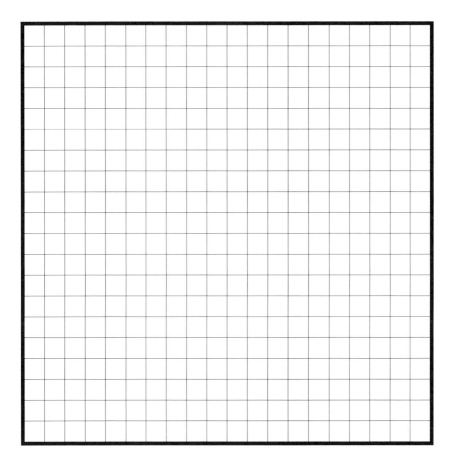

116 ODD-CUBE OUT

Imagine folding the shape below to form a six-sided cube. Which one of the five given cube pictures could not be the result?

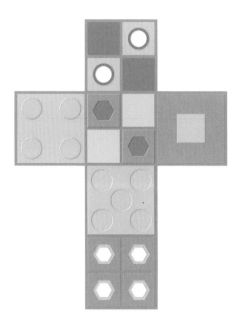

A

B

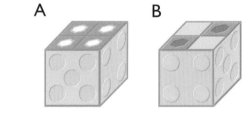

C

D

E

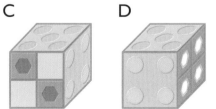

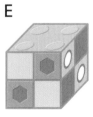

Solution on page 203

117 PAIRED UP

Join these images into four identical pairs.

A

E

B

F

C

G

D

H

Solution on page 204

118 TOUCHY

Place a letter in the range A to H into each empty square in such a way that no letter repeats in any row or column. Additionally, identical letters may not be in diagonally touching squares.

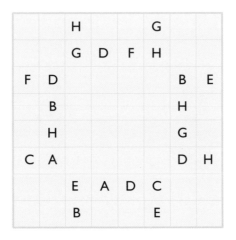

Solution on page 204

119 SHAPE LINK

Draw a series of separate paths, each connecting a pair of identical shapes. No more than one path can enter any square, and paths can only travel horizontally or vertically between squares.

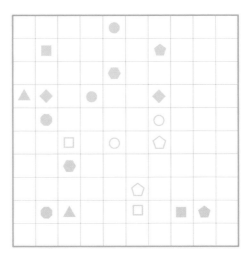

Solution on page 204

120 NUMBER DARTS

Form each of the given totals by choosing one number from each ring of the dartboard, so that those three numbers sum to the desired total.

TOTALS:	56
	75
	90

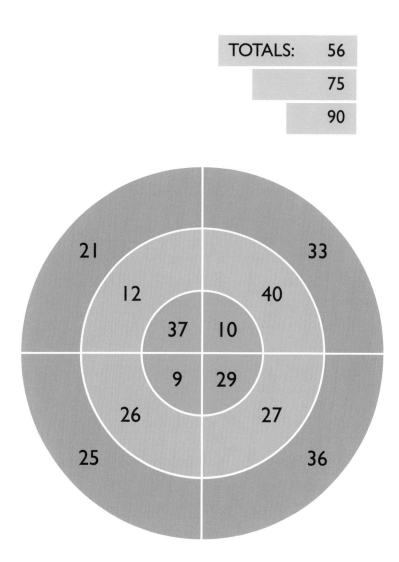

Solution on page 204

121 SHADING IT

Colour or shade in the regions formed by these shapes in whatever pattern or design you like. It's entirely up to you.

SPOT THE DIFFERENCE

Can you find all 8 differences between these two images?

Solution on page 205

123 CUBE COUNTING

How many cubes have been used to build the structure shown? You should assume that all 'hidden' cubes are present, and that it started off as a perfect 5x5x5 arrangement of cubes before any cubes were removed. There are no floating cubes.

Solution on page 204

124 NUMBER ANAGRAMS

Use all five numbers and all four basic mathematical signs, +, -, x and ÷ (once each), to reach each of the three targets in turn. You can use as many brackets as you want, but you cannot create any fractional (non-integer) numbers during your calculation.

1   4   5   12   75

TARGETS:

A: 38   B: 221   C: 447

Solution on page 204

3D SUDOKU

Place 1 to 9 into each empty square, so no digit repeat in any row, column or black-lined 3x3 area. The rows and columns bend to follow the contours of the 3D shape, starting and ending at either the edge of the puzzle or at a thick bold line.

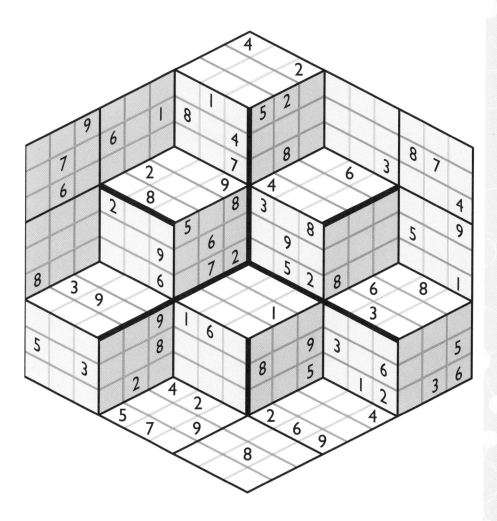

Solution on page 205

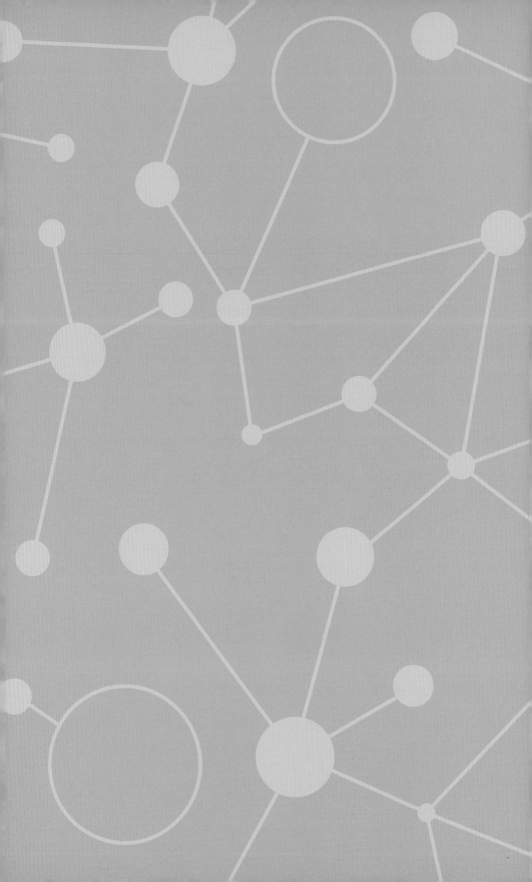

CHAPTER 6
MINDFULNESS

CHAPTER 6
MINDFULNESS

Back in chapter 3, we looked at the importance of being able to clear your mind and focus on the task in hand, although, of course, that's often more easily said than done. So, if you are struggling to minimise distracting thoughts that can make it harder to focus on a task, what can you do?

One option is to try various mindfulness techniques. Broadly speaking, these involve temporarily clearing in order to create a sense of calm. Based on ancient meditation practices, they can be used to help calm your mind and, in turn, your overall physical state. These are simple exercises which can be done anywhere, and where the objective is to set your distracting thoughts aside and focus purely on the here and now.

You could try the following simple mindfulness exercise, which uses breathing as a point of focus, for a few minutes:

- Find a quiet room where you can be free of distracting sounds, and that is neither too hot nor too cold. This might also be somewhere outside.
- Sit in a way that is comfortable for you, in a position you can maintain for five minutes or so.
- Close your eyes, if you feel comfortable doing so, and make sure your hands are resting comfortably.
- Consciously breathe in, then breathe out, at your normal speed. Pay attention to how your breath feels at this moment – for example, is it quick, or is it heavy? Do you notice any tension in your body?
- Continue to focus only on your breathing and ignore unrelated thoughts that arise as you concentrate. Let them come but, just as importantly, let them go without further inspection.
- Don't judge yourself harshly if your mind wanders – just take a

moment to bring your train of thought back to your breathing, without self-criticism.

There are, of course, many other ways to help yourself create a sense of peace, so it is worth finding a technique that works best for you. Gentle music in the background might help to create a relaxing atmosphere, for example, or it can be something to focus on instead of your breathing if you prefer. Prayer – if appropriate for you – may also have a similar calming effect.

It's also important to note that emptying your mind isn't something that needs to be a last resort – you don't need to wait until you feel you have to try it! In fact, practising mindfulness when you don't feel anxious or conflicted, or in a rush to complete a task, can help make it that much easier to summon a sense of calm later on. Just like a muscle we need to keep fit, the 'mindfulness muscle' can be exercised every day – even just for five minutes – so that you can then call upon tried and trusted calming techniques when you really need them.

126 SUDOKU

Place a digit from 1 to 9 into each empty square, so that no digit repeats in any row, column or bold-lined 3×3 box.

		4	8	6	5	9		
	8		7		2		6	
			1		9			
5	7						4	9
4								6
6	1						5	2
			4		1			
	5		2		7		3	
		1	6	9	3	2		

Solution on page 206

127 NO FOUR IN A ROW

Place either an 'X' or an 'O' into each empty square so that no lines of four or more 'X's or 'O's are formed in any direction, including diagonally.

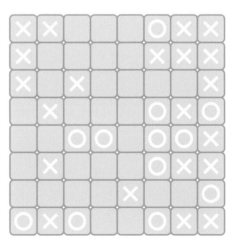

Solution on page 206

BRAIN CHAINS

Start with the number on the left of each chain, then apply each operation in turn until you reach the 'RESULT' box, writing your answer in the space provided. Try to complete the entire chain without using a calculator or making any written notes.

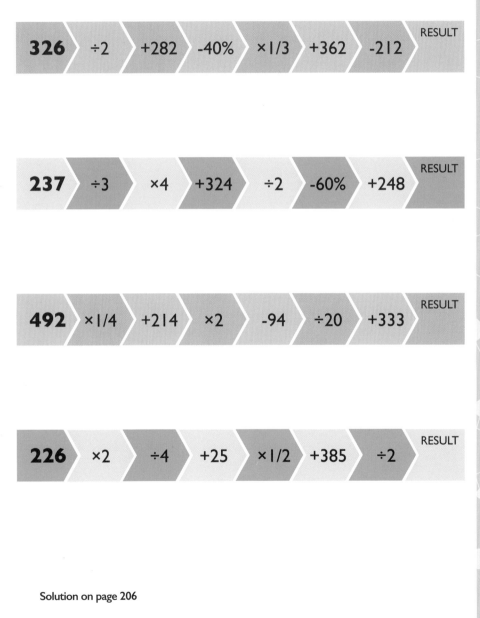

326 ÷2 +282 -40% ×1/3 +362 -212 RESULT

237 ÷3 ×4 +324 ÷2 -60% +248 RESULT

492 ×1/4 +214 ×2 -94 ÷20 +333 RESULT

226 ×2 ÷4 +25 ×1/2 +385 ÷2 RESULT

Solution on page 206

JOIN THE DOTS

Join these dots in whatever way you like, to create a doodle, abstract pattern or simple picture. If inspiration doesn't immediately strike, try drawing a few straight lines at random and then take a step back to see if the result reminds you of anything. Then continue in a similar vein.

MISSING CUBE FACE

Which of the five given options should replace the white face, so that all four cube images could then be different views of exactly the same cube?

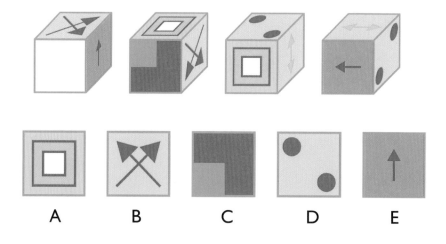

A   B   C   D   E

Solution on page 206

MAZE

Find your way from the top to the bottom of the maze. Some paths pass under or over other paths.

Solution on page 206

DOMINOES

Draw solid lines to divide the grid into a regular set of 0 to 6 dominoes, with exactly one of each domino. A '0' represents a blank on a traditional domino. Use the check-off chart to help you keep track of which dominoes you've already placed.

2	0	2	4	6	3	5	1
2	6	4	5	0	5	1	6
3	4	0	6	0	5	1	2
1	1	4	4	2	1	6	4
4	5	3	2	5	4	3	6
6	1	3	2	1	5	3	2
6	0	3	3	5	0	0	0

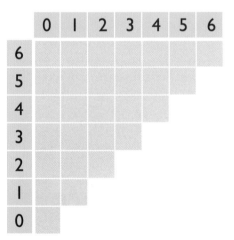

Solution on page 206

FENCES

Join all of the dots to form a single loop. The loop cannot cross or touch itself at any point. Only horizontal and vertical lines between dots are allowed. Some parts of the loop are already given.

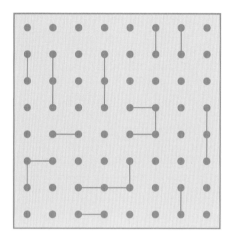

Solution on page 207

134 NUMBER PYRAMID

Complete this number pyramid by writing a number in each empty brick, so that each brick contains a value equal to the sum of the two bricks immediately beneath it.

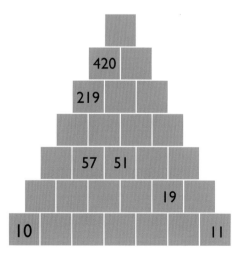

Solution on page 207

135 POETRY SLAM

Can you complete each of these two-line poems, in which only the first line is given? It's entirely up to you what you write, and they don't necessarily have to rhyme.

A pride of lionesses roamed,

....

They wandered through a distant land,

....

The stone was dark and cold and wet,

....

136 CUTTING PROBLEM

Draw along some of the dashed grid lines in order to divide this shape up into four regions. The regions must all be identical, although they may be rotated (but not reflected) relative to one another.

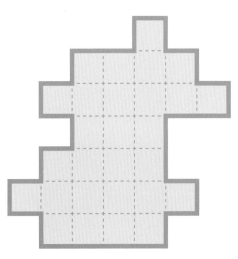

Solution on page 207

NUMBER PATH

Write a number in each empty square so that each number from 1 to 64 appears once in the grid. The numbers must form a path from 1 to 64, moving to a square one higher in value at each step as a king moves in chess: left, right, up, down or diagonally.

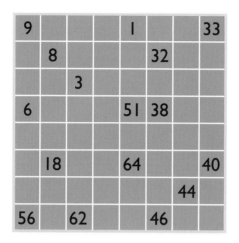

Solution on page 207

TRAIN TRACKS

Draw track pieces in some squares to complete a track that travels all the way from its entrance in the leftmost column to its exit in the bottom row. It can't otherwise exit the grid, and nor can it cross itself. Numbers outside the grid reveal the number of track pieces in each row and column. Every track piece must either go straight or turn a right-angled corner.

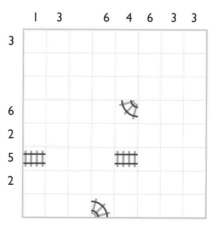

Solution on page 207

139 KAKURO

Place a number from 1 to 9 into each empty square, so that each continuous horizontal or vertical run of white squares adds up to the total given to its left or at its top, respectively. No number can repeat within any run.

Solution on page 207

140 PIXEL ART

Shade in your choice of squares on this canvas to create
a simple picture.

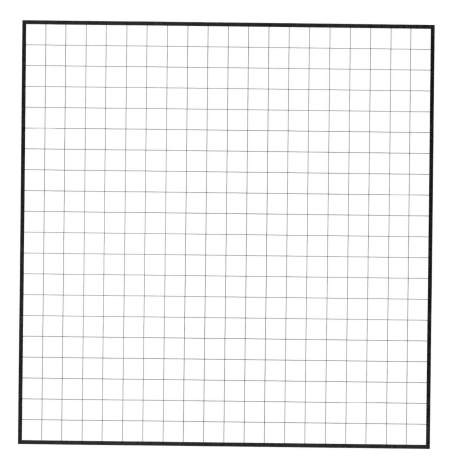

141 ODD-CUBE OUT

Imagine folding the shape below to form a six-sided cube. Which one of the five given cube pictures could not be the result?

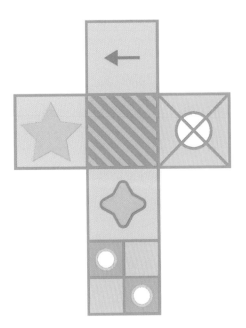

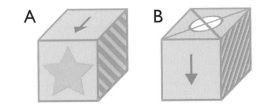

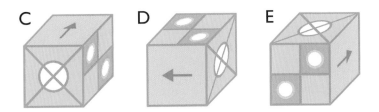

Solution on page 207

PAIRED UP

Join these images into four identical pairs.

A

E

B

F

C

G

D

H

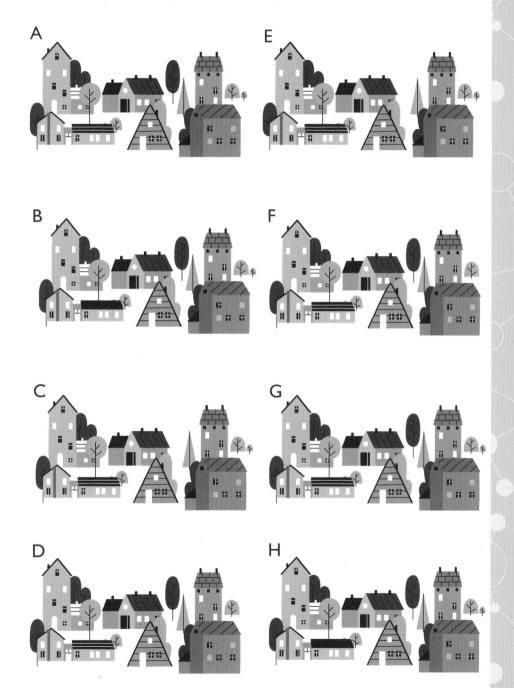

Solution on page 208

143 TOUCHY

Place a letter in the range A to H into each empty square in such a way that no letter repeats in any row or column. Additionally, identical letters may not be in diagonally touching squares.

	G	A	D	B			
H			B	C			F
E		F			H		G
F		B			C		H
A			F	H			B
		H	C	G	A		

Solution on page 208

144 SHAPE LINK

Draw a series of separate paths, each connecting a pair of identical shapes. No more than one path can enter any square, and paths can only travel horizontally or vertically between squares.

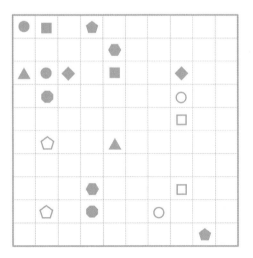

Solution on page 208

NUMBER DARTS

Form each of the given totals by choosing one number from each ring of the dartboard, so that those three numbers sum to the desired total.

TOTALS:	58
	72
	87

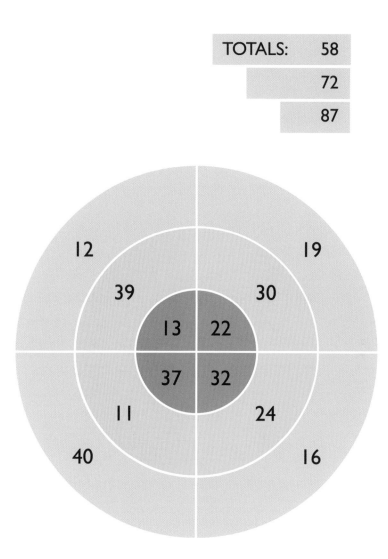

Solution on page 208

SHADING IT

Colour or shade in the regions formed by these shapes in whatever pattern or design you like. It's entirely up to you.

SPOT THE DIFFERENCE

Can you find all **8** differences between these two images?

Solution on page 209

148 CUBE COUNTING

How many cubes have been used to build the structure shown? You should assume that all 'hidden' cubes are present, and that it started off as a perfect 5x5x5 arrangement of cubes before any cubes were removed. There are no floating cubes.

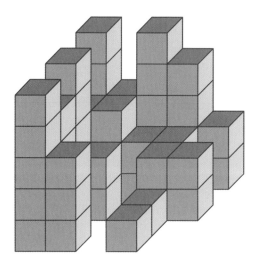

Solution on page 208

 # 149 NUMBER ANAGRAMS

Use all five numbers and all four basic mathematical signs, +, -, x and ÷ (once each), to reach each of the three targets in turn. You can use as many brackets as you want, but you cannot create any fractional (non-integer) numbers during your calculation.

TARGETS:

A: 27   B: 121   C: 407

Solution on page 208

150 3D SUDOKU

Place 1 to 9 into each empty square, so no digit repeat in any row, column or black-lined 3x3 area. The rows and columns bend to follow the contours of the 3D shape, starting and ending at either the edge of the puzzle or at a thick bold line.

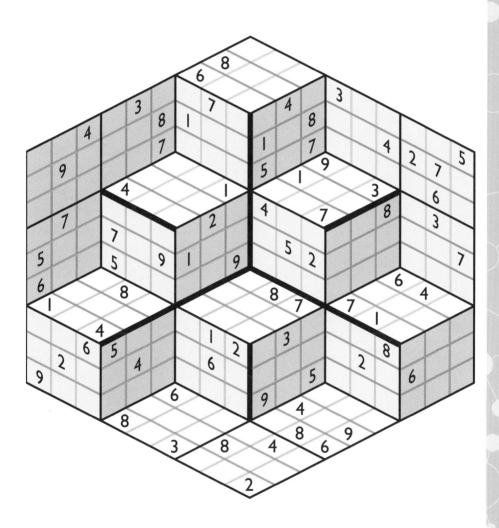

Solution on page 209

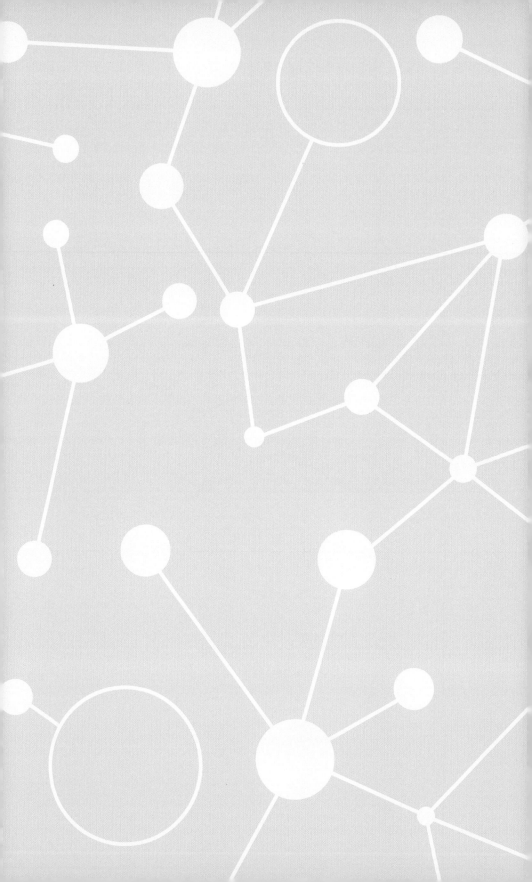

CHAPTER 7
SMART REASONING

CHAPTER 7
SMART REASONING

It can sometimes be tricky to know where to start when you have to make an important decision that can lead to an ability to proceed. How exactly do you decide the best job opportunity, study course to follow, or where to move to? This can be especially true when you need to draw a lot of information together at once, for decisions with a lot of complex variables to consider. How can you work out what information should be considered in making that decision and, even once you have that information, how do you know if it is reliable?

A good place to start is to look for things that might support a particular decision. For each of those things, you should then consider if it is something that is always true or that is open to interpretation. It might then also be sensible to look for reasons against making the same decision, and again to evaluate how solid each of those reasons is.

SAFETY IN NUMBERS
Sometimes it's obvious when information is too specific to be of general use. For example, if you looked closely at a single flower in your garden and saw that it had nine petals, you probably wouldn't conclude that all flowers of that type had nine petals, unless you had counted lots and lots of them and saw that this really did seem to be a rule. And yet, in so much of our lives, we often find ourselves making assumptions based on the flimsiest of evidence. Just because something is true once or twice, it doesn't mean that it will always be.

WHAT IF
Some problems can be best tackled by trying the 'what if' approach, which is essentially equivalent to guessing and then seeing what

happens. If you do this, carry through the thought process until you reach a conclusion or get stuck. This can sometimes help you get past a point where you're otherwise completely unsure how to proceed. You can always go back and try a different scenario to see what might happen in an alternative situation. In this way, you can often make progress much more quickly than by trying to think about all the different possibilities simultaneously.

This can also help with puzzles if you're not sure how to progress. Try a guess and see what happens – often, even if that guess turns out to be wrong, you learn something about the puzzle in the process that helps you get going again. Of course, choosing a sensible guess is also important – and picking a good 'either/or' choice will certainly help, as opposed to something with a long list of possible options.

CAREFUL CONCLUSIONS
Once you've reached a conclusion based on your decision-making and evidence-gathering, you may not yet be done, since it's just as important to make sure you've understood exactly what your conclusion means. In particular, it's important to remember that correlation does not equal causation – your result might just be a coincidence, rather than something that will generalise. Just because two things happen at the same time, it doesn't necessarily mean that they are connected. Suppose that sales of frisbees increase whenever rates of sunburn increase, and vice-versa. You could try to argue from this that that frisbees cause sunburn, or that sunburn makes you want to buy a frisbee. In this case, it's obvious that neither conclusion is sensible and that there is a third factor – good weather – involved but, in many cases, this type of false reasoning can be considerably harder to spot. So, it's important to always take care with your conclusions.

151 SUDOKU

Place a digit from 1 to 9 into each empty square, so that no digit repeats in any row, column or bold-lined 3×3 box.

Solution on page 210

152 NO FOUR IN A ROW

Place either an 'X' or an 'O' into each empty square so that no lines of four or more 'X's or 'O's are formed in any direction, including diagonally.

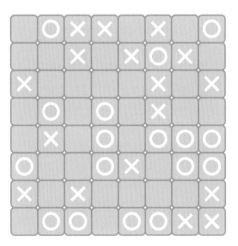

Solution on page 210

153 BRAIN CHAINS

Start with the number on the left of each chain, then apply each operation in turn until you reach the 'RESULT' box, writing your answer in the space provided. Try to complete the entire chain without using a calculator or making any written notes.

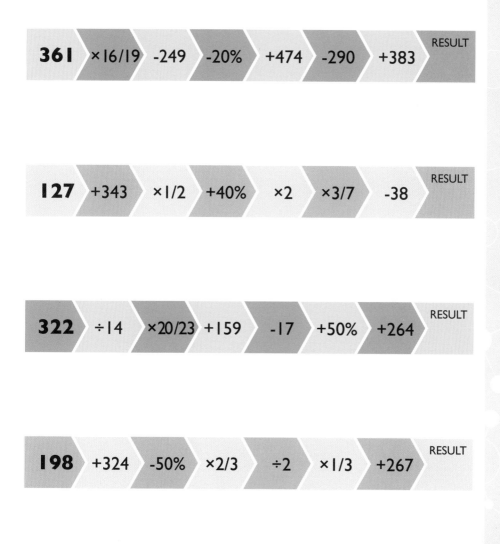

361 ×16/19 -249 -20% +474 -290 +383 RESULT

127 +343 ×1/2 +40% ×2 ×3/7 -38 RESULT

322 ÷14 ×20/23 +159 -17 +50% +264 RESULT

198 +324 -50% ×2/3 ÷2 ×1/3 +267 RESULT

Solution on page 210

154 JOIN THE DOTS

Join these dots in whatever way you like, to create a doodle, abstract pattern or simple picture. If inspiration doesn't immediately strike, try drawing a few straight lines at random and then take a step back to see if the result reminds you of anything. Then continue in a similar vein.

155 MISSING CUBE FACE

Which of the five given options should replace the white face, so that all four cube images could then be different views of exactly the same cube?

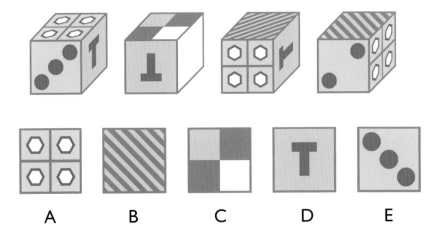

A   B   C   D   E

Solution on page 210

MAZE

Find your way from the top to the bottom of the maze. Some paths pass under or over other paths.

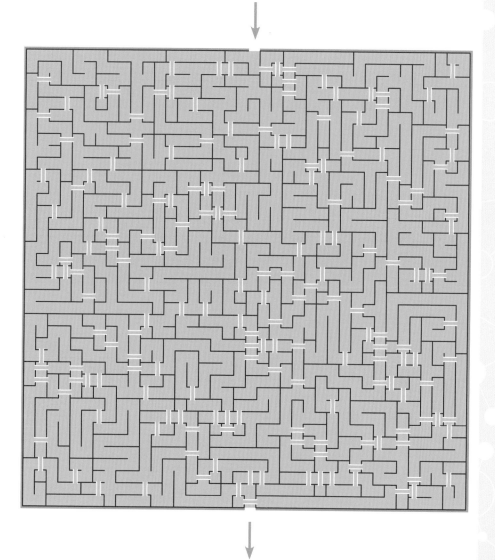

Solution on page 210

157 DOMINOES

Draw solid lines to divide the grid into a regular set of 0 to 6 dominoes, with exactly one of each domino. A '0' represents a blank on a traditional domino. Use the check-off chart to help you keep track of which dominoes you've already placed.

6	1	4	1	2	6	1	3
6	5	4	5	0	5	2	5
2	2	0	4	3	2	2	2
5	5	0	5	4	0	1	1
4	4	3	3	4	6	3	0
6	1	1	0	2	3	6	3
5	0	4	1	6	6	0	3

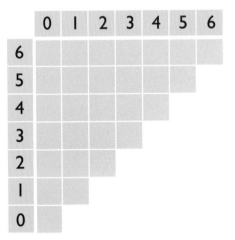

Solution on page 210

158 FENCES

Join all of the dots to form a single loop. The loop cannot cross or touch itself at any point. Only horizontal and vertical lines between dots are allowed. Some parts of the loop are already given.

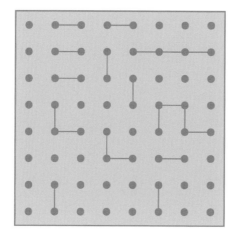

Solution on page 211

159 NUMBER PYRAMID

Complete this number pyramid by writing a number in each empty brick, so that each brick contains a value equal to the sum of the two bricks immediately beneath it.

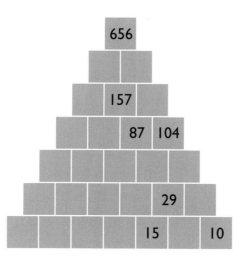

Solution on page 211

160 POETRY SLAM

Can you complete each of these two-line poems, in which only the
first line is given? It's entirely up to you what you write, and they don't
necessarily have to rhyme.

She wrote these words without a thought,

....

He tripped and fell and downwards went,

....

The shelves were bare and all around,

....

161 CUTTING PROBLEM

Draw along some of the dashed grid lines in order to divide this shape
up into four regions. The regions must all be identical, although they may
be rotated (but not reflected) relative to one another.

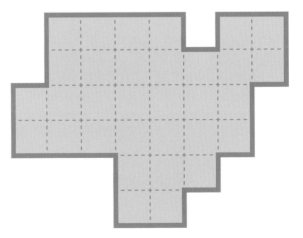

Solution on page 211

162 NUMBER PATH

Write a number in each empty square so that each number from 1 to 64 appears once in the grid. The numbers must form a path from 1 to 64, moving to a square one higher in value at each step as a king moves in chess: left, right, up, down or diagonally.

43						33
	41	40				
21				35		
	19					
				28		51
	15		59			2
	9		61		1	
	13	64				

Solution on page 211

Solution on page 211

163 TRAIN TRACKS

Draw track pieces in some squares to complete a track that travels all the way from its entrance in the leftmost column to its exit in the bottom row. It can't otherwise exit the grid, and nor can it cross itself. Numbers outside the grid reveal the number of track pieces in each row and column. Every track piece must either go straight or turn a right-angled corner.

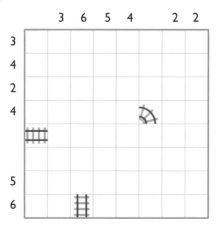

Solution on page 211

164 KAKURO

Place a number from 1 to 9 into each empty square, so that each continuous horizontal or vertical run of white squares adds up to the total given to its left or at its top, respectively. No number can repeat within any run.

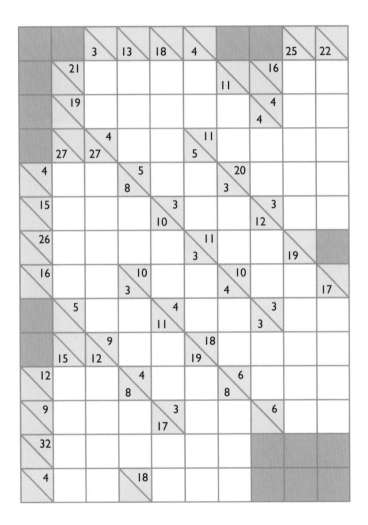

Solution on page 211

165 PIXEL ART

Shade in your choice of squares on this canvas to create a simple picture.

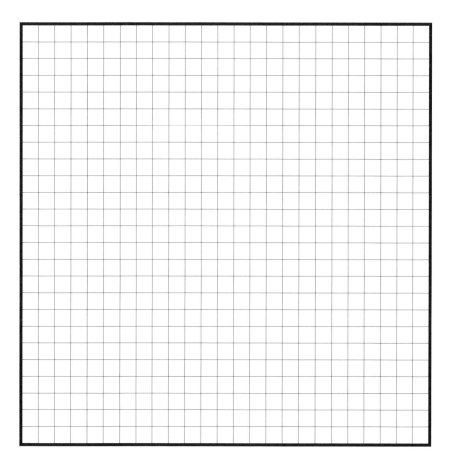

166 ODD-CUBE OUT

Imagine folding the shape below to form a six-sided cube. Which one of the five given cube pictures could not be the result?

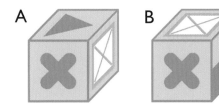

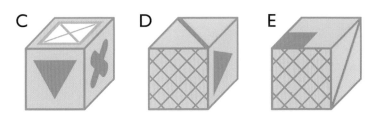

Solution on page 211

167 PAIRED UP

Join these images into four identical pairs.

A

B

C

D

E

F

G

H

Solution on page 212

168 TOUCHY

Place a letter in the range A to H into each empty square in such a way that no letter repeats in any row or column. Additionally, identical letters may not be in diagonally touching squares.

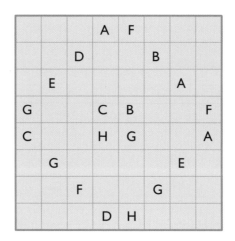

Solution on page 212

169 SHAPE LINK

Draw a series of separate paths, each connecting a pair of identical shapes. No more than one path can enter any square, and paths can only travel horizontally or vertically between squares.

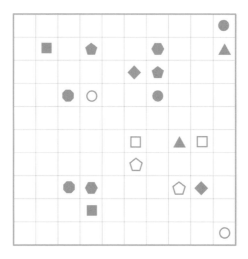

Solution on page 212

170 NUMBER DARTS

Form each of the given totals by choosing one number from each ring of the dartboard, so that those three numbers sum to the desired total.

TOTALS: 58

TOTALS:	58
	75
	85

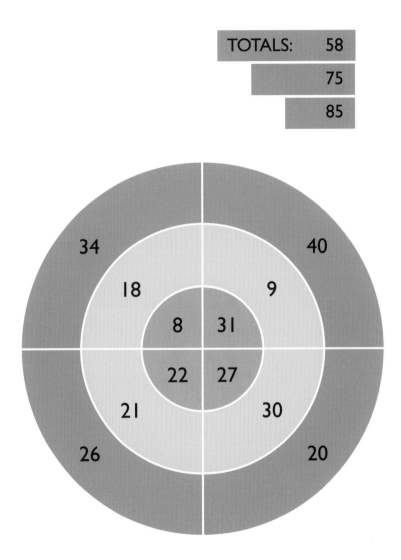

Solution on page 212

SHADING IT

Colour or shade in the regions formed by these shapes in whatever pattern or design you like. It's entirely up to you.

SPOT THE DIFFERENCE

Can you find all 8 differences between these two images?

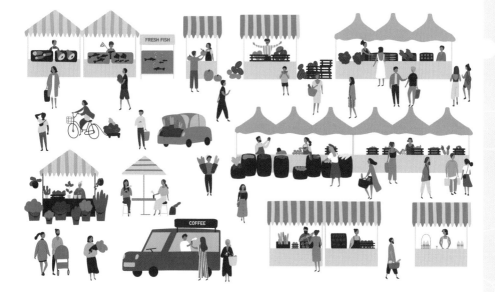

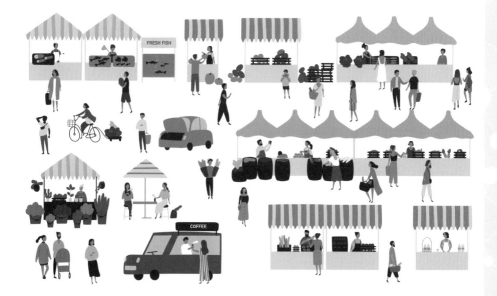

Solution on page 213

173 CUBE COUNTING

How many cubes have been used to build the structure shown? You should assume that all 'hidden' cubes are present, and that it started off as a perfect 6x6x6 arrangement of cubes before any cubes were removed. There are no floating cubes.

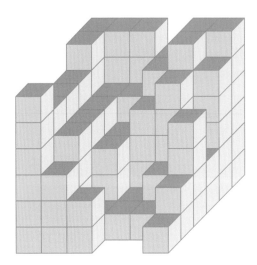

Solution on page 212

174 NUMBER ANAGRAMS

Use all five numbers and all four basic mathematical signs, +, -, x and ÷ (once each), to reach each of the three targets in turn. You can use as many brackets as you want, but you cannot create any fractional (non-integer) numbers during your calculation.

5   6   7   25   50

TARGETS:

A: 63   B: 132   C: 298

Solution on page 212

3D SUDOKU

Place 1 to 9 into each empty square, so no digit repeat in any row,
column or black-lined 3x3 area. The rows and columns bend to follow
the contours of the 3D shape, starting and ending at either the edge of
the puzzle or at a thick bold line.

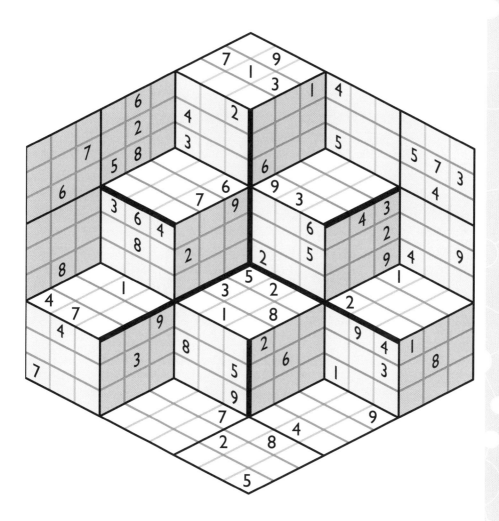

Solution on page 213

CHAPTER 8
LIFE-LONG LEARNING

CHAPTER 8
LIFE-LONG LEARNING

You've reached the start of the final chapter, so congratulations! It's likely that, along the way, you've challenged your brain to try many different things, learned some new skills and possibly even learned to find a sense of calm. So, what now?

Well, the good news is that your brain-training needn't stop once this chapter is complete. Looking after your brain is a life-long commitment, and what's been covered in this book is just a flavour of what you can continue to do every day to help keep your brain fit and active. Try setting aside just five minutes each day to clear your thoughts with a mindfulness technique, and spending another five minutes or so trying a puzzle or other task that you find properly challenging or novel. Your brain will thank you, since even a short brain workout each day is far better than none at all.

Don't forget that it's also important to look after your brain just as much as you would the rest of your body, to improve your odds of a healthy and fulfilling life. In fact, there's no reason that the two can't be combined. Joining a dance class is a good example, since learning a new dance routine is both a physical workout and a mind and memory workout too. Social activities, too, are virtually always a great boost for the brain, especially if they are new or unfamiliar – and, in particular, the importance of social contact in later life cannot be overstated. You might like to try volunteering, for example, or joining an evening class to learn an entirely new skill. You could also join a club or society as a great way to ensure that you'll make regular time to keep your brain busy – and even if it's a little intimidating to start with, both the activity itself and the associated social contact will be hugely good for your brain.

Once you've begun to deliberately incorporate brain fitness into your daily routine, it can develop into a healthy, life-long practice. To that end, here's a reminder of some of the most important brain-boosting tips, so that you can continue building your brain-training routine:

- Take time to clear out distractions – mental or otherwise – when you need to get something done, so that your brain can work at its best.
- Look carefully at facts and figures when you're making decisions, and use properly reasoned logic to make informed choices, rather than relying on gut instincts.
- Try something new every day, even if it's only a small change. Eat a new food, learn a new word, solve a different puzzle, or travel a different route.
- Take five minutes to practise a mindfulness technique that you've found helpful, to help bring a sense of calm when needed that can help you focus without distractions.
- Most importantly, keep it going! A little bit of brain-training every day will keep your mind active, your memory sharp and your brain happy.

176 SUDOKU

Place a digit from 1 to 9 into each empty square, so that no digit repeats in any row, column or bold-lined 3×3 box.

	4			6			1	
7	3						9	8
8								4
			3		1			
	7	2				9	6	
		1	2	5	9	8		
	2		4		7		3	

Solution on page 214

177 NO FOUR IN A ROW

Place either an 'X' or an 'O' into each empty square so that no lines of four or more 'X's or 'O's are formed in any direction, including diagonally.

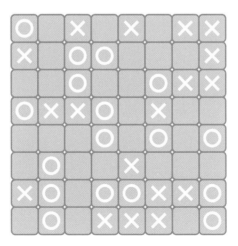

Solution on page 214

BRAIN CHAINS

Start with the number on the left of each chain, then apply each operation in turn until you reach the 'RESULT' box, writing your answer in the space provided. Try to complete the entire chain without using a calculator or making any written notes.

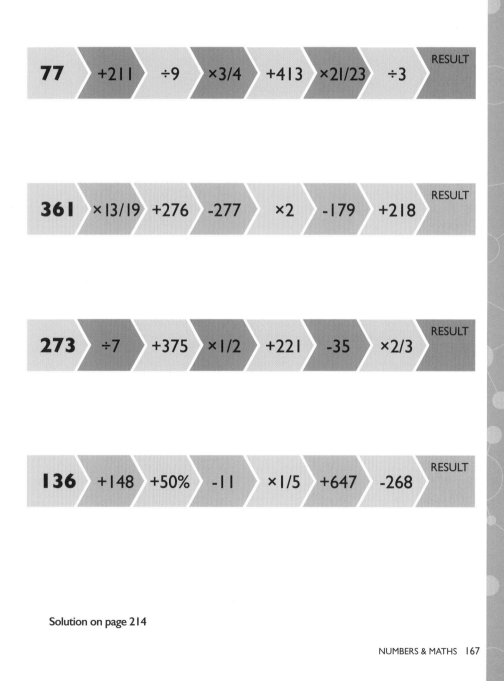

77 | +211 | ÷9 | ×3/4 | +413 | ×21/23 | ÷3 | RESULT

361 | ×13/19 | +276 | -277 | ×2 | -179 | +218 | RESULT

273 | ÷7 | +375 | ×1/2 | +221 | -35 | ×2/3 | RESULT

136 | +148 | +50% | -11 | ×1/5 | +647 | -268 | RESULT

Solution on page 214

179 JOIN THE DOTS

Join these dots in whatever way you like, to create a doodle, abstract pattern or simple picture. If inspiration doesn't immediately strike, try drawing a few straight lines at random and then take a step back to see if the result reminds you of anything. Then continue in a similar vein.

180 MISSING CUBE FACE

Which of the five given options should replace the white face, so that all four cube images could then be different views of exactly the same cube?

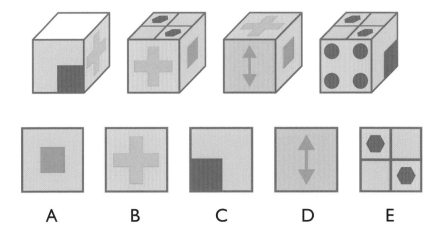

A   B   C   D   E

Solution on page 214

MAZE

Find your way from the top to the bottom of the maze. Some paths pass under or over other paths.

Solution on page 214

182 DOMINOES

Draw solid lines to divide the grid into a regular set of 0 to 6 dominoes, with exactly one of each domino. A '0' represents a blank on a traditional domino. Use the check-off chart to help you keep track of which dominoes you've already placed.

4	1	6	1	1	3	3	4
2	3	4	2	5	0	5	1
4	5	3	0	5	6	3	3
3	1	6	0	2	5	0	4
4	0	3	5	2	5	6	4
0	0	1	2	6	1	2	2
5	6	6	1	4	2	0	6

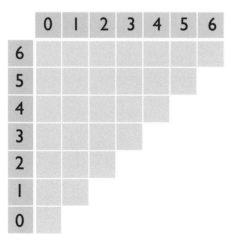

Solution on page 214

183 FENCES

Join all of the dots to form a single loop. The loop cannot cross or touch itself at any point. Only horizontal and vertical lines between dots are allowed. Some parts of the loop are already given.

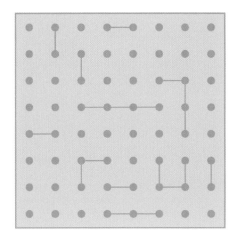

Solution on page 215

184 NUMBER PYRAMID

Complete this number pyramid by writing a number in each empty brick, so that each brick contains a value equal to the sum of the two bricks immediately beneath it.

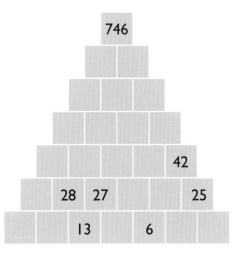

Solution on page 215

POETRY SLAM

Can you complete each of these two-line poems, in which only the first line is given? It's entirely up to you what you write, and they don't necessarily have to rhyme.

I wandered through the crowded room,

....

The hall was packed; they looked at me,

....

The mist came down without a sound,

....

 CUTTING PROBLEM

Draw along some of the dashed grid lines in order to divide this shape up into four regions. The regions must all be identical, although they may be rotated (but not reflected) relative to one another.

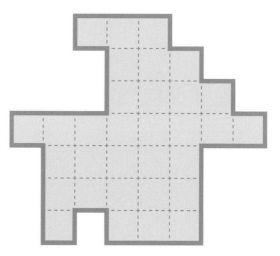

Solution on page 215

187 NUMBER PATH

Write a number in each empty square so that each number from 1 to 64 appears once in the grid. The numbers must form a path from 1 to 64, moving to a square one higher in value at each step as a king moves in chess: left, right, up, down or diagonally.

	1			9		15
		6	5	8		
	41				17	
			36			
		47				23
			49	54		
	58	64			27	
59			63		51	28

Solution on page 215

188 TRAIN TRACKS

Draw track pieces in some squares to complete a track that travels all the way from its entrance in the leftmost column to its exit in the bottom row. It can't otherwise exit the grid, and nor can it cross itself. Numbers outside the grid reveal the number of track pieces in each row and column. Every track piece must either go straight or turn a right-angled corner.

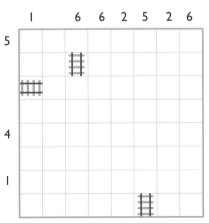

Solution on page 215

KAKURO

Place a number from 1 to 9 into each empty square, so that each continuous horizontal or vertical run of white squares adds up to the total given to its left or at its top, respectively. No number can repeat within any run.

Solution on page 215

PIXEL ART

Shade in your choice of squares on this canvas to create a simple picture.

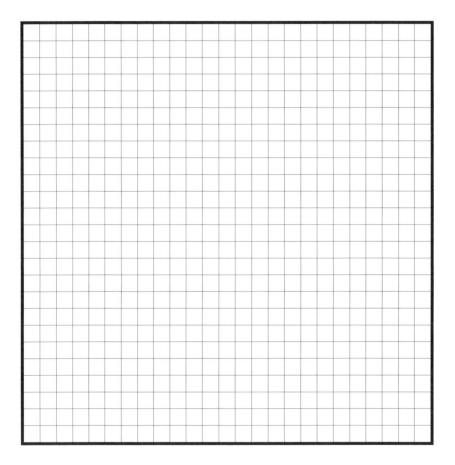

ODD-CUBE OUT

Imagine folding the shape below to form a six-sided cube. Which one of the five given cube pictures could not be the result?

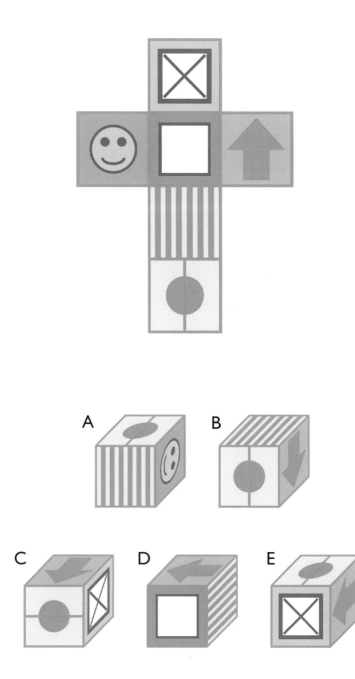

Solution on page 215

192 PAIRED UP

Join these images into four identical pairs.

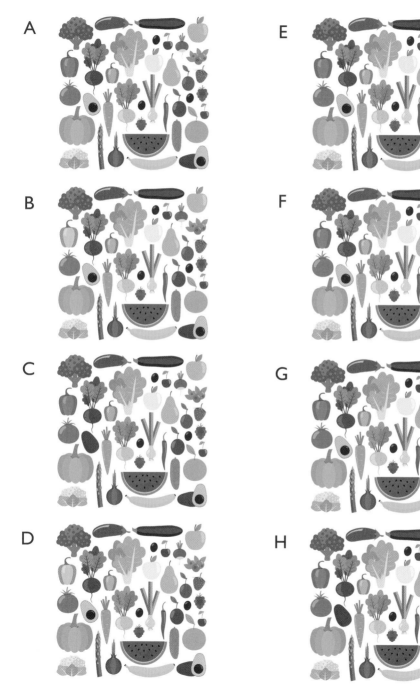

A

B

C

D

E

F

G

H

Solution on page 216

193 TOUCHY

Place a letter in the range A to H into each empty square in such a way that no letter repeats in any row or column. Additionally, identical letters may not be in diagonally touching squares.

Solution on page 216

194 SHAPE LINK

Draw a series of separate paths, each connecting a pair of identical shapes. No more than one path can enter any square, and paths can only travel horizontally or vertically between squares.

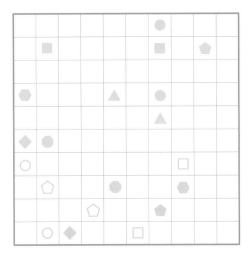

Solution on page 216

195 NUMBER DARTS

Form each of the given totals by choosing one number from each ring of the dartboard, so that those three numbers sum to the desired total.

TOTALS: 65
78
88

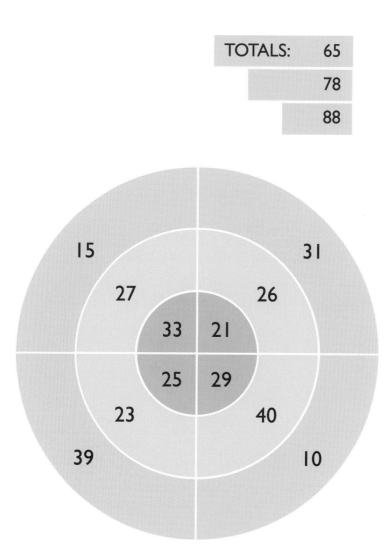

Solution on page 216

SHADING IT

Colour or shade in the regions formed by these shapes in whatever pattern or design you like. It's entirely up to you.

SPOT THE DIFFERENCE

Can you find all 8 differences between these two images?

Solution on page 217

CUBE COUNTING

How many cubes have been used to build the structure shown? You should assume that all 'hidden' cubes are present, and that it started off as a perfect 6x6x6 arrangement of cubes before any cubes were removed. There are no floating cubes.

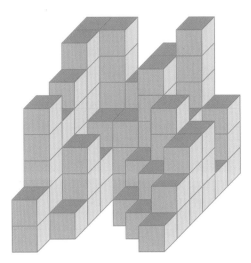

Solution on page 216

NUMBER ANAGRAMS

Use all five numbers and all four basic mathematical signs, +, -, x and ÷ (once each), to reach each of the three targets in turn. You can use as many brackets as you want, but you cannot create any fractional (non-integer) numbers during your calculation.

3   8   10   25   100

TARGETS:

A: 59   B: 231   C: 914

Solution on page 216

200 3D SUDOKU

Place 1 to 9 into each empty square, so no digit repeat in any row, column or black-lined 3x3 area. The rows and columns bend to follow the contours of the 3D shape, starting and ending at either the edge of the puzzle or at a thick bold line.

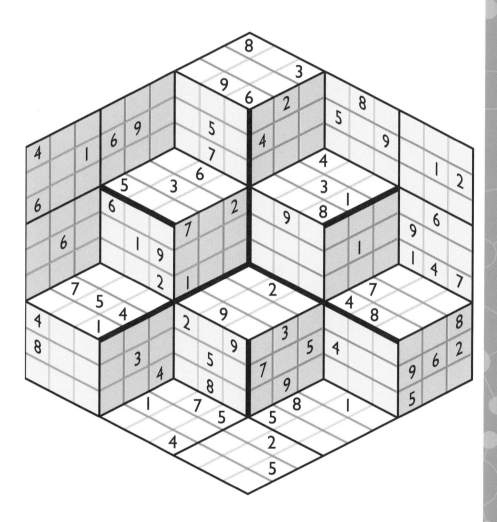

Solution on page 217

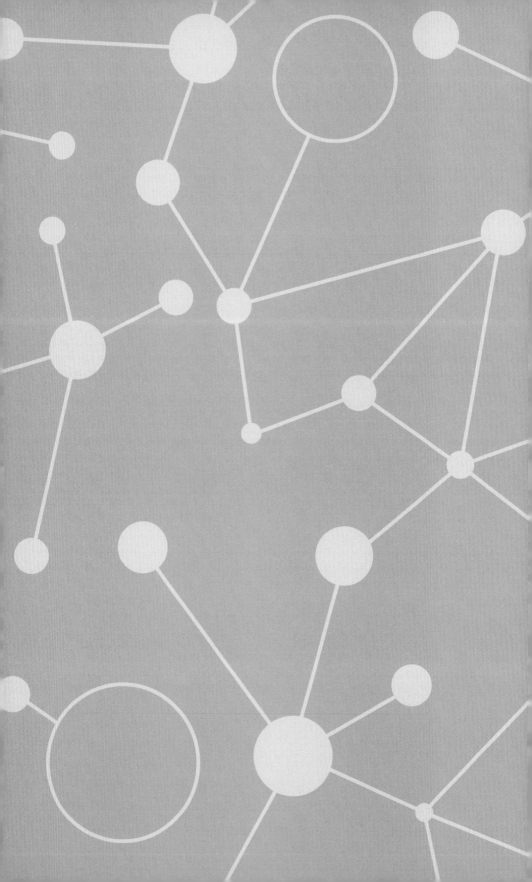

SOLUTIONS

CHAPTER 1
SOLUTIONS

1: Sudoku

8	1	4	5	3	6	3	9	7
7	6	5	2	9	8	3	1	4
3	2	9	7	4	1	6	8	5
1	8	2	6	5	3	7	4	9
5	7	3	9	2	4	8	6	1
4	9	6	8	1	7	5	3	2
9	3	7	4	8	5	1	2	6
6	4	8	1	7	2	9	5	3
2	5	1	3	6	9	4	7	8

2: No Four in a row

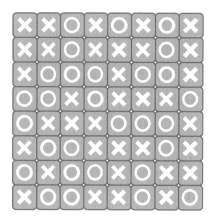

3: Brain chains

A. 17

B. 144

C. 48

D. 158

5: Missing cube face

B

6: Maze

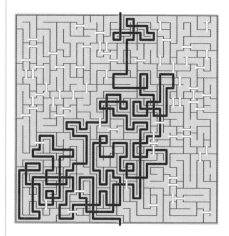

7: Dominoes

2	2	0	0	0	1	5	3
0	4	2	2	2	3	1	1
5	6	6	5	4	1	0	0
1	6	5	5	4	6	3	2
6	5	6	1	4	6	6	0
3	0	3	4	4	4	2	1
4	5	3	3	2	5	3	1

8: Fences

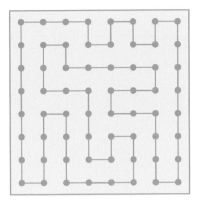

13: Train tracks

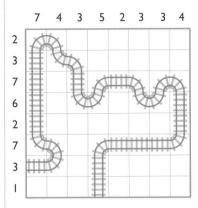

9: Number pyramid

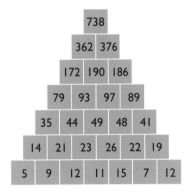

14: Kakuro

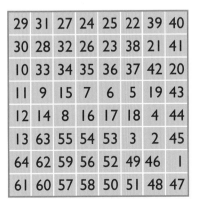

11: Cutting problem

12: Number path

29	31	27	24	25	22	39	40
30	28	32	26	23	38	21	41
10	33	34	35	36	37	42	20
11	9	15	7	6	5	19	43
12	14	8	16	17	18	4	44
13	63	55	54	53	3	2	45
64	62	59	56	52	49	46	1
61	60	57	58	50	51	48	47

16: Odd-cube out

A

17: Paired up

A&F

B&H

C&G

D&E

18: Touchy

H	B	D	E	C	G	A	F
D	A	H	G	B	F	C	E
F	E	C	A	H	D	B	G
G	H	B	D	E	A	F	C
A	C	E	F	G	B	H	D
B	F	G	H	D	C	E	A
E	D	A	C	F	H	G	B
C	G	F	B	A	E	D	H

19: Shape link

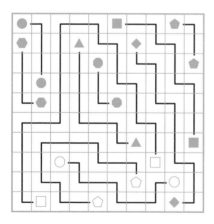

20: Number darts

60 = 28 + 20 + 12

67 = 36 + 19 + 12

82 = 24 + 40 + 18

23: Cubes counting

There are 32 cubes: 3 on the topmost layer; 6 on the second layer; 10 on the third layer; and 13 on the bottom layer

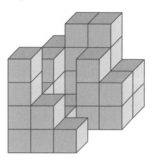

24: Number anagrams

A:

15 + 9 = 24

8 - 6 = 2

24 ÷ 2 = 12

12 × 3 = 36

B:

8 × 6 = 48

48 + 9 = 57

15 ÷ 3 = 5

57 - 5 = 52

C:

9 ÷ 3 = 3

8 - 3 = 5

15 + 6 = 21

21 × 5 = 105

22: Spot the difference

25: 3D sudoku

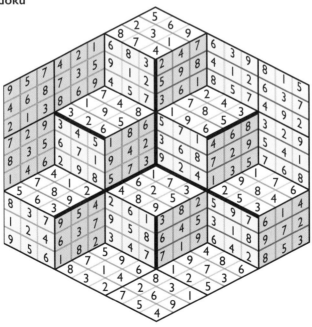

CHAPTER 2
SOLUTIONS

26: Sudoku

4	5	2	6	3	8	7	1	9
6	1	7	4	5	9	8	2	3
3	9	8	1	7	2	5	4	6
5	2	4	7	1	6	3	9	8
7	3	9	2	8	4	1	6	5
8	6	1	5	9	3	4	7	2
1	7	6	3	2	5	9	8	4
2	8	3	9	4	1	6	5	7
9	4	5	8	6	7	2	3	1

27: No Four in a row

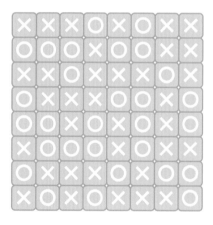

28: Brain chains

A. 49

B. 64

C. 77

D. 80

30: Missing cube face

B

31: Maze

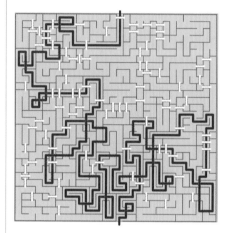

32: Dominoes

0	1	1	6	0	5	2	3
2	2	4	4	6	1	0	0
5	5	3	4	0	2	3	5
3	6	6	1	0	0	3	6
5	3	2	4	4	5	4	0
1	6	6	4	2	5	1	3
4	2	2	6	1	1	5	3

33: Fences

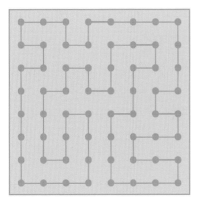

34: Number pyramid

			754			
		375		379		
	190		185		194	
100		90		95		99
54	46	44	51	48		

28	26	20	24	27	21
13	15	11	9	15	12	9

36: Cutting problem

37: Number path

9	10	5	12	13	14	45	44
8	6	11	4	15	46	43	48
7	18	17	16	3	42	47	49
19	25	26	27	28	2	41	50
24	20	55	56	1	29	51	40
23	21	57	54	30	52	38	39
22	62	60	58	53	31	37	35
64	63	61	59	32	33	34	36

38: Train tracks

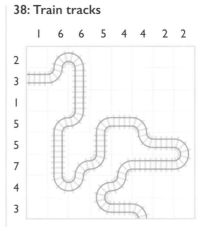

39: Kakuro

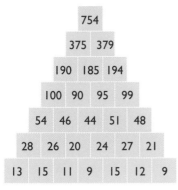

41: Odd-cube out

A

42: Paired up

A&F

C&E

D&G

B&H

43: Touchy

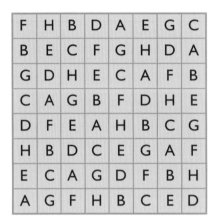

F	H	B	D	A	E	G	C
B	E	C	F	G	H	D	A
G	D	H	E	C	A	F	B
C	A	G	B	F	D	H	E
D	F	E	A	H	B	C	G
H	B	D	C	E	G	A	F
E	C	A	G	D	F	B	H
A	G	F	H	B	C	E	D

44: Shape link

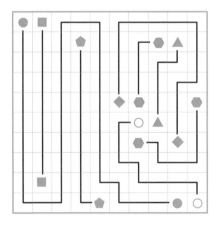

45: Number darts

45 = 13 + 17 + 15

53 = 25 + 9 + 19

68 = 20 + 9 + 39

48: Cube counting

There are 27 cubes: 3 on the topmost layer; 5 on the second layer; 8 on the third layer; and 11 on the bottom layer

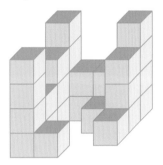

49: Number anagrams

A:

11 + 7 = 18

25 × 18 = 450

450 ÷ 10 = 45

45 - 4 = 41

B:

11 - 10 = 1

7 ÷ 1 = 7

25 × 4 = 100

100 + 7 = 107

C:

11 - 7 = 4

4 ÷ 4 = 1

25 + 1 = 26

26 × 10 = 260

47: Spot the difference

50: 3D sudoku

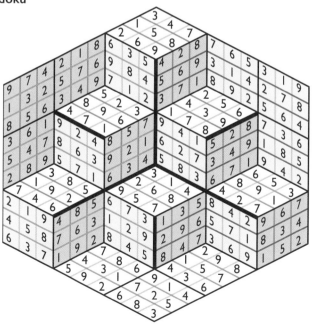

CHAPTER 3
SOLUTIONS

51: Sudoku

6	9	7	8	3	2	5	1	4
2	5	4	6	1	7	9	3	8
8	1	3	5	4	9	2	7	6
4	2	5	3	6	8	1	9	7
7	8	6	9	2	1	3	4	5
9	3	1	7	5	4	8	6	2
5	6	2	1	7	3	4	8	9
1	4	9	2	8	6	7	5	3
3	7	8	4	9	5	6	2	1

52: No Four in a row

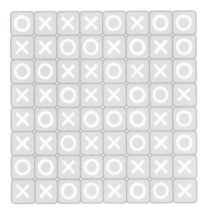

53: Brain chains

A. 131

B. 39

C. 112

D. 138

55: Missing cube face

C

56: Maze

57: Dominoes

3	3	5	3	0	6	1	2
2	0	1	6	0	1	2	4
6	5	2	6	4	6	3	3
4	2	2	1	4	0	4	5
4	5	5	1	2	5	2	1
1	4	5	6	3	6	4	0
5	3	0	6	1	0	3	0

58: Fences

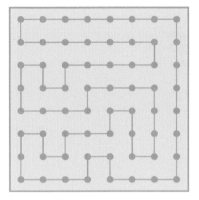

59: Number pyramid

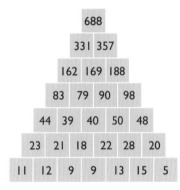

```
              688
          331   357
       162   169   188
     83    79    90    98
   44    39    40    50    48
 23   21   18   22   28   20
11  12   9    9   13   15   5
```

61: Cutting problem

62: Number path

8	9	4	3	44	43	42	39
10	7	2	5	45	41	40	38
11	13	6	1	31	46	35	37
12	15	14	32	30	34	47	36
16	26	28	29	33	48	53	52
25	17	27	61	59	54	49	51
24	22	18	60	62	58	55	50
23	21	20	19	63	64	57	56

63: Train tracks

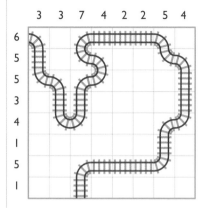

64: Kakuro

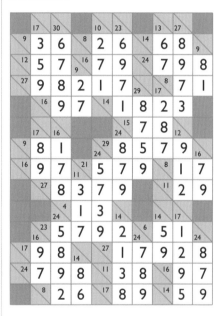

66: Odd-cube out

E

67: Paired up

A&D

B&H

C&F

E&G

68: Touchy

A	H	B	G	C	E	F	D
F	G	A	E	B	D	C	H
C	B	D	H	F	A	E	G
H	F	C	A	E	G	D	B
E	D	G	F	H	B	A	C
B	A	E	D	G	C	H	F
D	C	H	B	A	F	G	E
G	E	F	C	D	H	B	A

69: Shape link

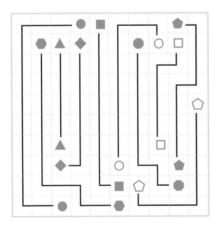

70: Number darts

48 = 9 + 20 + 19

66 = 28 + 17 + 21

77 = 28 + 13 + 36

73: Cube counting

There are 46 cubes: 6 on the topmost layer; 8 on the second layer; 14 on the third layer; and 18 on the bottom layer

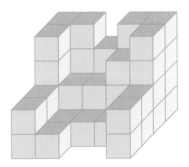

74: Number anagrams

A:

9 - 8 = 1

5 ÷ 1 = 5

10 × 2 = 20

20 + 5 = 25

B:

8 ÷ 2 = 4

10 + 4 = 14

14 × 5 = 70

70 - 9 = 61

C:

9 + 5 = 14

14 × 8 = 112

10 ÷ 2 = 5

112 - 5 = 107

72: Spot the difference

75: 3D sudoku

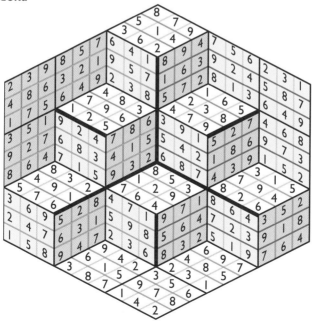

CHAPTER 4
SOLUTIONS

76: Sudoku

3	4	2	6	9	1	7	8	5
8	5	1	4	7	3	2	9	6
6	9	7	8	5	2	3	4	1
4	3	5	1	2	7	8	6	9
7	8	9	3	6	4	1	5	2
2	1	6	5	8	9	4	3	7
5	6	3	7	1	8	9	2	4
9	7	8	2	4	6	5	1	3
1	2	4	9	3	5	6	7	8

77: No Four in a row

X	O	X	X	X	O	X	O	X
O	X	O	X	X	X	O	X	O
O	X	X	X	O	X	X	O	O
X	X	O	O	X	O	O	X	X
O	O	X	O	X	X	X	O	X
X	X	X	O	X	O	O	O	X
X	O	O	X	O	O	X	O	O
X	X	O	O	X	X	O	O	O

78: Brain chains

A. 61

B. 180

C. 128

D. 94

80: Missing cube face

E

81: Maze

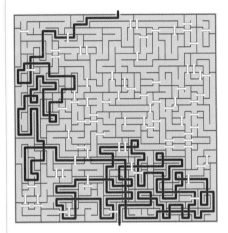

82: Dominoes

6	2	5	4	6	3	4	3
0	5	6	6	2	1	1	3
0	1	0	4	4	3	3	4
5	0	2	6	1	6	0	4
6	2	2	0	5	2	1	3
4	4	1	2	0	6	2	3
5	3	1	5	5	5	1	0

83: Fences

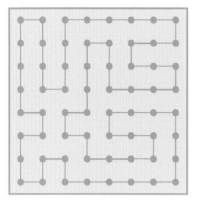

84: Number pyramid

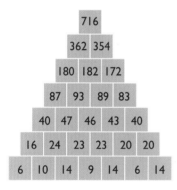

		716				
362	354
180	182	172
87	93	89	83
40	47	46	43	40
16	24	23	23	20	20
6	10	14	9	14	6	14

86: Cutting problem

87: Number path

40	39	38	37	34	33	19	18
43	41	36	35	32	20	17	16
44	42	30	31	21	12	13	15
45	46	9	29	11	22	26	14
47	8	7	10	28	27	23	25
48	6	3	4	64	63	62	24
49	2	5	54	55	61	60	59
1	50	51	52	53	56	57	58

88: Train tracks

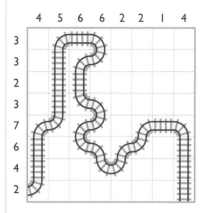

89: Kakuro

	23	13	16	9	16		21	9
34	8	4	9	6	7	15\10	9	6
19	6	2	7	3	1	13\14	3	8	2
16	9	7	9\	20\29	8	5	2	4	1
	15\33	6	9	13\24	9	4	34\
	20\15	7	1	8	4	7\	1	6	7\
29	5	9	2	7	6	15\	7	4
17	9	8	8\	5	2	1	6\8	4	2
4	1	3	24\	21\	7	3	2	8	1
	10\	6	4	9\	5	2	1	9
	17\8	9\	8	1	14\14	9	5	15\	21\
34	6	4	9	8	7	17\	14\6	5	9
6	2	1	3	34\	6	9	4	7	8
12	9	3		18\	1	8	2	3	4

91: Odd-cube out

A

199

92: Paired up

A&G

B&E

C&H

D&F

93: Touchy

H	B	A	D	G	E	C	F
D	E	C	B	A	F	H	G
G	A	D	F	H	C	E	B
F	C	G	A	E	B	D	H
B	D	H	C	F	G	A	E
A	G	F	E	D	H	B	C
E	H	B	G	C	A	F	D
C	F	E	H	B	D	G	A

94: Shape link

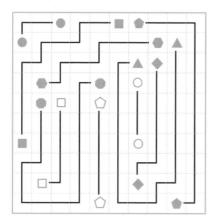

95: Number darts

58 = 8 + 34 + 16

74 = 14 + 37 + 23

88 = 31 + 34 + 23

98: Cube counting

There are 38 cubes: 2 on the topmost layer; 8 on the second layer; 11 on the third layer; and 17 on the bottom layer

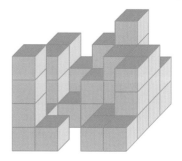

99: Number anagrams

A:

50 ÷ 10 = 5

9 + 5 = 14

14 - 6 = 8

8 × 3 = 24

B:

50 - 10 = 40

40 + 9 = 49

49 × 6 = 294

294 ÷ 3 = 98

C:

50 × 9 = 450

450 - 10 = 440

6 ÷ 3 = 2

440 + 2 = 442

97: Spot the difference

100: 3D sudoku

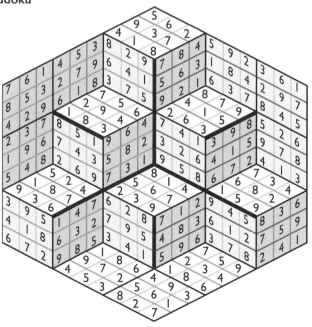

CHAPTER 5
SOLUTIONS

101: Sudoku

2	4	9	7	1	5	3	8	6
6	3	1	8	9	4	2	7	5
7	5	8	6	3	2	4	1	9
9	7	4	2	5	1	6	3	8
8	2	6	9	7	3	5	4	1
3	1	5	4	8	6	9	2	7
1	8	2	3	6	9	7	5	4
5	6	3	1	4	7	8	9	2
4	9	7	5	2	8	1	6	3

102: No Four in a row

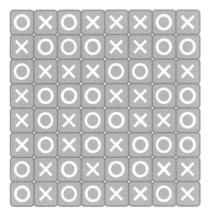

103: Brain chains

A. 37

B. 97

C. 63

D. 103

105: Missing cube face

A

106: Maze

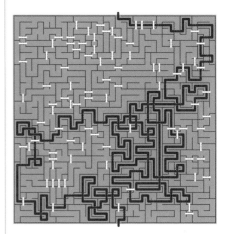

107: Dominoes

6	1	1	4	2	3	1	4
0	2	2	6	2	5	4	0
3	6	5	6	2	1	5	0
3	1	2	4	4	3	0	4
5	1	3	0	3	0	1	4
1	6	0	3	2	5	5	4
6	3	0	5	6	6	5	2

108: Fences

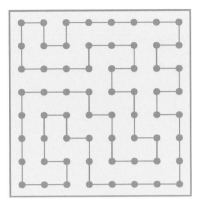

113: Train tracks

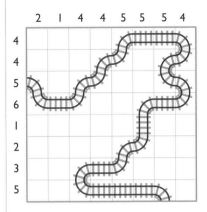

109: Number pyramid

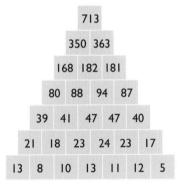

			713			
		350		363		
	168	182		181		
80	88	94		87		

Pyramid values:

- 713
- 350, 363
- 168, 182, 181
- 80, 88, 94, 87
- 39, 41, 47, 47, 40
- 21, 18, 23, 24, 23, 17
- 13, 8, 10, 13, 11, 12, 5

114: Kakuro

16	4	3	23		12	11
8	1	2	6	3	2	1
9	7	3	1	2	9	7
8	7	1		5	2	1	3
3	1			3	4	
3	1		9	7	1	2
2	3	1		8	1	2
2	9		4	2	7	3	1
1	2	7		4	2	3	
3	9	8	7		1	3	
2	1				2	1
5	1	8	3		2	1	3
1	2		5	8	7	3	9
2	3		2	7	9	1	

111: Cutting problem

112: Number path

35	37	38	5	4	21	20	19
36	34	39	3	6	22	17	18
33	31	40	7	2	16	23	14
32	41	30	1	8	24	15	13
44	29	42	27	25	9	10	12
45	43	28	51	26	56	64	11
48	46	50	52	55	63	57	59
47	49	53	54	62	61	60	58

116: Odd-cube out

A

117: Paired up

A&C

B&G

D&F

E&H

118: Touchy

A	F	H	C	B	G	E	D
B	E	G	D	F	H	C	A
F	D	C	H	G	A	B	E
G	B	A	E	C	D	H	F
E	H	D	B	A	F	G	C
C	A	F	G	E	B	D	H
H	G	E	A	D	C	F	B
D	C	B	F	H	E	A	G

119: Shape link

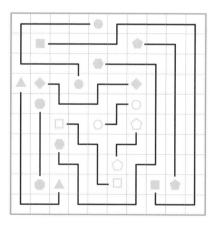

120: Number darts

56 = 9 + 26 + 21

75 = 10 + 40 + 25

90 = 29 + 40 + 21

123: Cube counting

There are 66 cubes: 6 on the topmost layer; 9 on the second layer; 12 on the third layer; 17 on the fourth layer; and 22 on the bottom layer

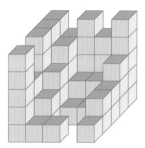

124: Number anagrams

A:

75 × 4 = 300

5 + 1 = 6

300 ÷ 6 = 50

50 - 12 = 38

B:

75 × 12 = 900

900 ÷ 4 = 225

225 - 5 = 220

220 + 1 = 221

C:

5 + 1 = 6

75 × 6 = 450

12 ÷ 4 = 3

450 - 3 = 447

122: Spot the difference

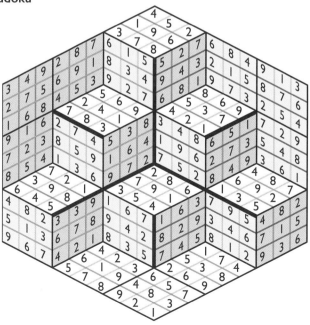

125: 3D sudoku

CHAPTER 6
SOLUTIONS

126: Sudoku

7	3	4	8	6	5	9	2	1
1	8	9	7	4	2	5	6	3
2	6	5	1	3	9	4	8	7
5	7	2	3	1	6	8	4	9
4	9	3	5	2	8	7	1	6
6	1	8	9	7	4	3	5	2
3	2	7	4	5	1	6	9	8
9	5	6	2	8	7	1	3	4
8	4	1	6	9	3	2	7	5

127: No Four in a row

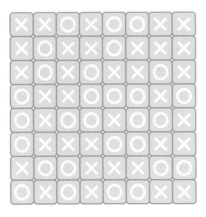

128: Brain chains

A. 239

B. 376

C. 362

D. 227

130: Missing cube face

C

131: Maze

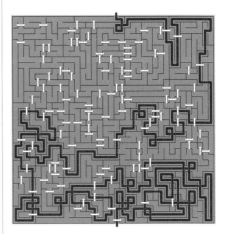

132: Dominoes

2	0	2	4	6	3	5	1
2	6	4	5	0	5	1	6
3	4	0	6	0	5	1	2
1	1	4	4	2	1	6	4
4	5	3	2	5	4	3	6
6	1	3	2	1	5	3	2
6	0	3	3	5	0	0	0

133: Fences

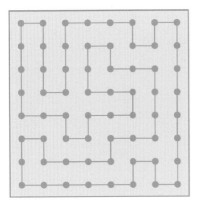

138: Train tracks

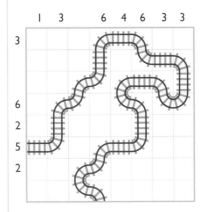

134: Number pyramid

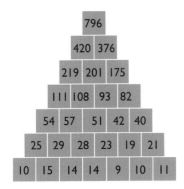

139: Kakuro

	7	16	15	27	8		17	25	
32	5	7	9	8	3	16	7	9	
25	2	9	6	7	1	4 19	3	1	
	16	17	34 26	9	4	7	6	8	5
13	7	1	2	3	12 11	2	1	5	4
23	9	8	6	4	3	1	3 28	2	1
4	3	1	23	8	9	6	26		
14	5	9	18	9		16	7	9	
14	14 23	8	5	1		4	1	3	7
13	9	4	17 28	9	8	23 18	9	8	6
12	5	2	4	1	15 21	3	5	6	1
	26	1	7	3	9	6	17	4	6
16	7	9	18	4	2	8	3	1	
17	9	8	30	8	7	9	1	5	

136: Cutting problem

137: Number path

9	11	12	13	1	35	34	33
10	8	4	2	14	36	32	31
7	5	3	15	25	26	37	30
6	22	16	24	51	38	27	29
21	17	23	53	52	50	39	28
20	18	54	59	64	49	41	40
19	55	58	63	60	48	44	42
56	57	62	61	47	46	45	43

141: Odd-cube out

E

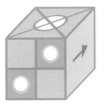

142: Paired up

A&G

C&E

B&H

D&F

143: Touchy

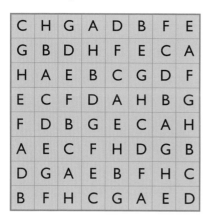

C	H	G	A	D	B	F	E
G	B	D	H	F	E	C	A
H	A	E	B	C	G	D	F
E	C	F	D	A	H	B	G
F	D	B	G	E	C	A	H
A	E	C	F	H	D	G	B
D	G	A	E	B	F	H	C
B	F	H	C	G	A	E	D

144: Shape link

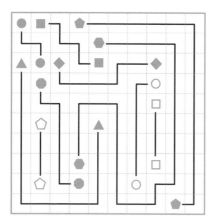

145: Number darts

58 = 22 + 24 + 12

72 = 32 + 24 + 16

87 = 32 + 39 + 16

148: Cube counting

There are 54 cubes: 4 on the topmost layer; 6 on the second layer; 10 on the third layer; 16 on the fourth layer; and 18 on the bottom layer

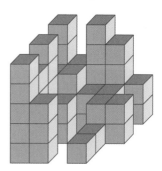

149: Number anagrams

A:

12 - 10 = 2

50 × 2 = 100

100 + 8 = 108

108 ÷ 4 = 27

B:

50 × 10 = 500

500 ÷ 4 = 125

125 - 12 = 113

113 + 8 = 121

C:

50 × 8 = 400

400 + 10 = 410

12 ÷ 4 = 3

410 - 3 = 407

147: Spot the difference

150: 3D sudoku

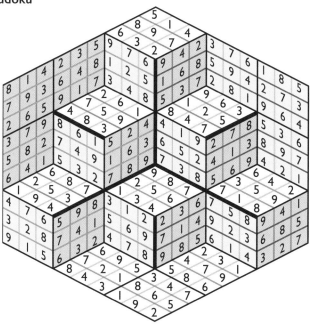

CHAPTER 7
SOLUTIONS

151: Sudoku

1	6	8	7	4	2	3	5	9
9	2	3	5	8	1	6	7	4
4	7	5	9	6	3	8	2	1
7	4	1	8	3	6	2	9	5
5	3	6	2	1	9	7	4	8
2	8	9	4	7	5	1	6	3
6	5	2	1	9	8	4	3	7
8	9	7	3	2	4	5	1	6
3	1	4	6	5	7	9	8	2

152: No Four in a row

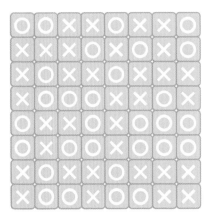

153: Brain chains

A. 611

B. 244

C. 507

D. 296

155: Missing cube face

E

156: Maze

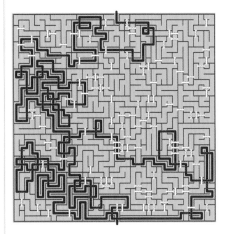

157: Dominoes

6	1	4	1	2	6	1	3
6	5	4	5	0	5	2	5
2	2	0	4	3	2	2	2
5	5	0	5	4	0	1	1
4	4	3	3	4	6	3	0
6	1	1	0	2	3	6	3
5	0	4	1	6	6	0	3

158: Fences

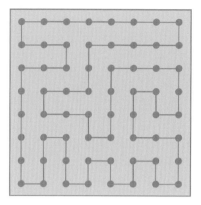

163: Train tracks

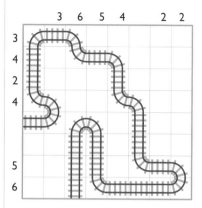

159: Number pyramid

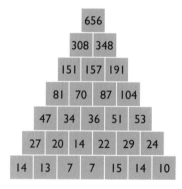

161: Cutting problem

162: Number path

43	44	45	39	38	37	32	33
42	41	40	46	36	48	34	31
21	20	18	26	47	35	49	30
22	19	25	17	27	4	29	50
23	24	7	16	5	28	3	51
10	8	15	6	59	60	52	2
11	9	14	62	61	58	1	53
12	13	63	64	57	56	55	54

164: Kakuro

		³\	¹³\	¹⁸\	⁴\			²⁵\	²²\
	²¹\	1	9	8	3	\¹¹	¹⁶\	9	7
	¹⁹\	2	3	5	1	8	⁴\⁴	1	3
	²⁷\	⁴\²⁷	1	3	\¹¹₅	3	1	5	2
⁴\	²⁷\	3	1	\⁵₈	2	3	\²⁰₃	3	8	9
¹⁵\	8	6	1	\³₁₀	2	1	\³₁₂	2	1
²⁶\	9	8	7	2	\¹¹₃	2	9	\¹⁹	
¹⁶\	7	9	\¹⁰₃	8	2	\¹⁰₄	3	7	\¹⁷
	⁵\	3	2	\⁴₁₁	1	3	\³₃	2	1
	¹⁵\	¹²\	1	8	\¹⁸₁₉	1	2	6	9
¹²\	9	3	\⁴₈	3	1	\⁶₈	1	3	2
⁹\	2	6	1	\³₁₇	2	1	\⁶	1	5
³²\	1	2	7	8	9	5			
⁴\	3	1	\¹⁸	9	7	2			

166: Odd-cube out

C

167: Paired up

A&H

B&G

C&F

D&E

168: Touchy

E	C	B	A	F	H	G	D
H	A	D	G	E	B	F	C
B	E	H	F	D	C	A	G
G	D	A	C	B	E	H	F
C	F	E	H	G	D	B	A
D	G	C	B	A	F	E	H
A	H	F	E	C	G	D	B
F	B	G	D	H	A	C	E

169: Shape link

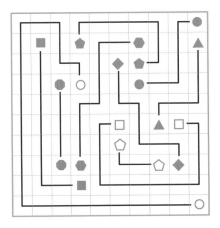

170: Number darts

58 = 8 + 30 + 20

75 = 31 + 18 + 26

85 = 27 + 18 + 40

173: Cube counting

There are 133 cubes: 8 on the topmost layer; 15 on the second layer; 22 on the third layer; 25 on the fourth layer; 29 on the fifth layer; and 34 on the bottom layer

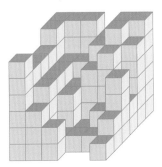

174: Number anagrams

A:

50 ÷ 25 = 2

6 - 2 = 4

5 + 4 = 9

9 × 7 = 63

B:

25 + 7 = 32

50 ÷ 5 = 10

32 - 10 = 22

22 × 6 = 132

C:

50 × 6 = 300

300 - 7 = 293

25 ÷ 5 = 5

293 + 5 = 298

172: Spot the difference

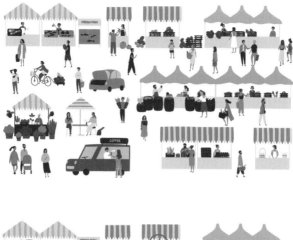

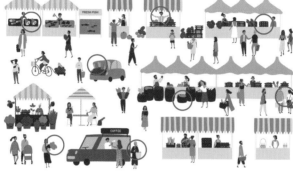

175: 3D sudoku

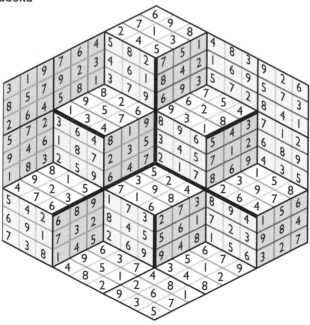

CHAPTER 8
SOLUTIONS

176: Sudoku

2	4	9	7	6	8	3	1	5
7	3	6	1	4	5	2	9	8
8	1	5	9	2	3	6	7	4
6	8	4	3	9	1	7	5	2
5	9	3	6	7	2	4	8	1
1	7	2	5	8	4	9	6	3
3	6	1	2	5	9	8	4	7
4	5	7	8	3	6	1	2	9
9	2	8	4	1	7	5	3	6

177: No Four in a row

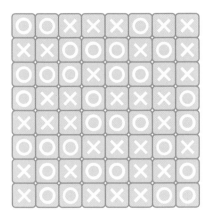

178: Brain chains

A. 133

B. 531

C. 262

D. 462

180: Missing cube face

E

181: Maze

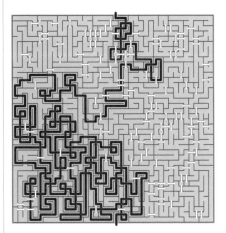

182: Dominoes

4	1	6	1	1	3	3	4
2	3	4	2	5	0	5	1
4	5	3	0	5	6	3	3
3	1	6	0	2	5	0	4
4	0	3	5	2	5	6	4
0	0	1	2	6	1	2	2
5	6	6	1	4	2	0	6

183: Fences

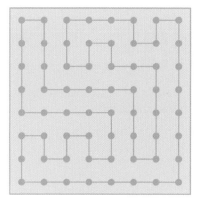

188: Train tracks

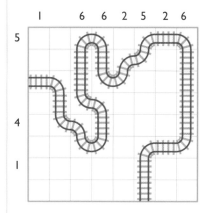

184: Number pyramid

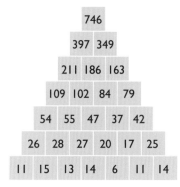

189: Kakuro

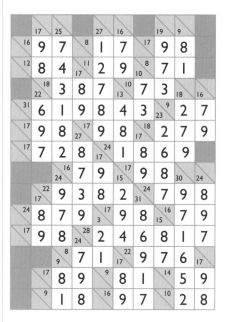

186: Cutting problem

187: Number path

2	1	4	7	10	9	14	15
40	3	6	5	8	11	16	13
39	41	37	35	18	17	12	21
42	38	46	36	34	19	20	22
43	45	47	48	33	32	25	23
44	57	56	49	54	26	31	24
60	58	64	55	50	53	27	30
59	61	62	63	52	51	29	28

191: Odd-cube out

C

215

192: Paired up

A&F

B&D

C&H

E&G

193: Touchy

G	B	A	E	D	H	F	C
D	F	G	C	B	E	A	H
E	H	B	F	A	D	C	G
A	G	D	H	C	B	E	F
H	C	E	A	F	G	D	B
B	D	F	G	E	C	H	A
F	E	C	B	H	A	G	D
C	A	H	D	G	F	B	E

194: Shape link

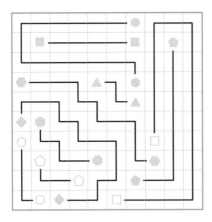

195: Number darts

65 = 29 + 26 + 10

78 = 21 + 26 + 31

88 = 33 + 40 + 15

198: Cube counting

There are 92 cubes: 4 on the topmost layer; 8 on the second layer; 11 on the third layer; 18 on the fourth layer; 23 on the fifth layer; and 28 on the bottom layer

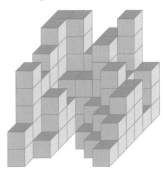

199: Number anagrams

A:

$100 \times 10 = 1000$

$1000 + 3 = 1003$

$25 - 8 = 17$

$1003 \div 17 = 59$

B:

$100 \div 10 = 10$

$10 - 3 = 7$

$25 + 8 = 33$

$33 \times 7 = 231$

C:

$100 + 10 = 110$

$110 \times 25 = 2750$

$2750 - 8 = 2742$

$2742 \div 3 = 914$

197: Spot the difference

200: 3D sudoku

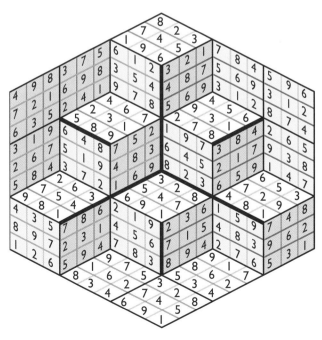

NOTES

NOTES

NOTES

NOTES

NOTES